POLICE PROBLEM-SOLVING MODELS AND THEORIES

DEDICATIONS

Steve Wadley: *for Lois and Emily*

Sharda Murria: *for Vin, Rohan and Rian*

Laura Riley: *for Craig, Terri, Andrew and Laurence*

To order our books please go to our website www.criticalpublishing.com or contact our distributor Ingram Publisher Services, telephone 01752 202301 or email IPSUK.orders@ingramcontent.com. Details of bulk order discounts can be found at www.criticalpublishing.com/delivery-information.

Our titles are also available in electronic format: for individual use via our website and for libraries and other institutions from all the major ebook platforms.

POLICE PROBLEM-SOLVING MODELS AND THEORIES

THE PROFESSIONAL POLICING CURRICULUM IN PRACTICE

STEVEN WADLEY, LAURA RILEY AND SHARDA MURRIA

SERIES EDITOR: TONY BLOCKLEY

CRITICAL PUBLISHING

First published in 2023 by Critical Publishing Ltd

All rights reserved. No part of this publication may be reproduced, stored in a retrieval system, or transmitted in any form or by any means, electronic, mechanical, photocopying, recording or otherwise, without prior permission in writing from the publisher.

The authors have made every effort to ensure the accuracy of information contained in this publication, but assume no responsibility for any errors, inaccuracies, inconsistencies and omissions. Likewise, every effort has been made to contact copyright holders. If any copyright material has been reproduced unwittingly and without permission the Publisher will gladly receive information enabling them to rectify any error or omission in subsequent editions.

Copyright © 2023 Sharda Murria, Laura Riley and Steven Wadley

British Library Cataloguing in Publication Data
A CIP record for this book is available from the British Library

ISBN: 978-1-915713-27-8

This book is also available in the following e-book formats:
EPUB ISBN: 978-1-915713-28-5
Adobe e-book ISBN: 978-1-915713-29-2

The rights of Sharda Murria, Laura Riley and Steven Wadley to be identified as the Authors of this work have been asserted by them in accordance with the Copyright, Design and Patents Act 1988.

Text and cover design by Out of House Limited
Project management by Newgen Publishing UK

Critical Publishing
3 Connaught Road
St Albans
AL3 5RX

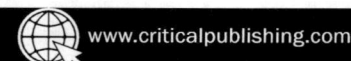

Printed on FSC accredited paper

CONTENTS

About the series editor and authors — vi

Foreword by the series editor — viii

Chapter 1: Neighbourhood policing — 1

Chapter 2: Hot spot policing — 27

Chapter 3: Predictive policing — 45

Chapter 4: Rational Choice Theory — 65

Chapter 5: Situational crime prevention — 87

Chapter 6: Partnership working in crime prevention — 113

Sample answers — 133

References — 161

Index — 175

ABOUT THE SERIES EDITOR

TONY BLOCKLEY

Tony Blockley is the lead for policing at Leeds Trinity University, responsible for co-ordinating policing higher education, including developing programmes and enhancing the current provision in line with the Police Education Qualification Framework (PEQF) and supporting the College of Policing. He served within policing for over 30 years, including a role as Chief Superintendent and Head of Crime.

ABOUT THE AUTHORS

DR SHARDA MURRIA

Dr Sharda Murria is a lecturer in criminology and policing at Birmingham City University. She is a socio-legal scholar, and her PhD examines the use of body-worn videos in stop and search, focusing on the balance between legality and legitimacy. She is passionate about community engagement and scrutiny, promoting fair and lawful policing.

LAURA RILEY

Laura Riley is a lecturer in criminology and policing at Birmingham City University and a PhD researcher, examining how social networks promote desistance from sexual offending. Her teaching focuses on vulnerabilities, diversity, abuse detection and prevention, appropriate responses to disclosure, multi-agency working, ethics and the impact on mental health. She is passionate about social justice, promoting ethical policing, desistance and safeguarding vulnerable individuals.

STEVEN WADLEY

Steven Wadley is course leader for the BSc in Professional Policing and the BA Criminology and Associated Pathways at Birmingham City University, teaching at both undergraduate and postgraduate levels. He is working towards a PhD examining the impact of working as a special constable alongside being a full-time professional policing student, focusing on mental health, well-being and academic attainment.

FOREWORD

Police professionalism has seen significant developments over recent years, including the implementation of the Vision 2025 and the establishment of the Police Education Qualification Framework (PEQF). There is no doubt that policing has become complex, and this complexity and its associated challenges are increasing day by day with greater scrutiny, expectations and accountability. The educational component of police training and development therefore allows officers to gain a greater understanding and appreciation of the theories and activities associated with high-quality policing provision.

The scholastic element of the Vision 2025 provides an opportunity to engage in meaningful insight and debate around some of the most sensitive areas of policing while also taking lessons from the past to develop the service for the future. While there are many books and articles on numerous subjects associated with policing, this new series – *The Professional Policing Curriculum in Practice* – provides an insightful opportunity to start that journey. It distils the key concepts and topics within policing into an accessible format, combining theory and practice to provide you with a secure basis of knowledge and understanding.

Policing is now a degree-level entry profession, which has provided a unique opportunity to develop fully up-to-date books for student and trainee police officers that focus on the content of the PEQF curriculum, are tailored specifically to the new pre-join routes, and reflect the diversity and complexity of twenty-first-century society. Each book is stand-alone, but they also work together to layer information as you progress through your programme. The pedagogical features of the books have been carefully designed to improve your understanding and critical thinking skills within the context of policing. They include learning objectives, case studies, evidence-based practice examples, critical thinking and reflective activities, and summaries of key concepts. Each chapter also includes a guide to further reading, meaning you don't have to spend hours researching to find that piece of information you are looking for.

Police problem-solving models and theories are a significant aspect of policing and an essential tool in understanding crime to initiate a suitable response. Exploring the role of community and neighbourhood policing is crucial to engaging communities and understanding their differences in order to provide an effective policing service.

Understanding some of the key policing models, including hot spot, predictive and situational crime prevention, allows the reader to develop a depth of knowledge that will assist them in their future policing roles. Including the various theories relating to crime prevention and partnership working provides for the greater efficiency and effectiveness of any policing response. The development of knowledge in these areas provides a critical underpinning for policing, enabling the practical application of knowledge within the operational setting.

Having been involved in policing for over 40 years, the benefits of these books are obvious to me: I see them becoming the go-to guides for the PEQF curriculum across all the various programmes associated with the framework while also having relevance for more experienced officers.

Professor Tony Blockley
Discipline Head: Policing
Leeds Trinity University

CHAPTER 1
NEIGHBOURHOOD POLICING

LEARNING OBJECTIVES

AFTER READING THIS CHAPTER YOU WILL BE ABLE TO:

- describe the evolution of community and neighbourhood policing;

- apply various neighbourhood policing approaches, including engaging communities, problem solving and targeting activity;

- understand and apply the Scanning, Analysis, Response, Assessment (SARA) model to neighbourhood policing issues;

- explore practical guidance on partnership working with communities and partner organisations to achieve neighbourhood policing aims.

INTRODUCTION

You will most likely be familiar with the phrase '*the police are the public and the public are the police*' from the Peelian principles. The premise that a good relationship with the public is beneficial to the police forms the basis of community policing in England and Wales. Community policing is the umbrella term given to decentralised policing activities which focus on empowering communities by allowing them to define local policing priorities and work in partnership with the police and other organisations to address these issues. Although there is no single definition of community policing, its broad nature has allowed it to be flexibly applied to a range of diverse communities in various different circumstances.

Neighbourhood policing is a more recent concept which developed from community policing and is explored in detail through this chapter. It is considered the 'bedrock' of British policing and continues to be an essential aspect of contemporary policing. In this chapter you will learn about different approaches to neighbourhood policing, together with practical ideas and advice on how to implement these approaches.

> **Neighbourhood policing is an approach that seeks to increase contact between the police and the public in defined local geographic areas in order to make the work of the police more responsive to the needs of local people.**
>
> (Quinton and Morris, 2008, p 1)

THE EVOLUTION OF NEIGHBOURHOOD POLICING

THE COMMUNITY POLICING AND REASSURANCE POLICING MODEL

> *Community policing is the delivery of police services through a customer-focused approach, utilising partnerships to maximise community resources in a problem-solving format to prevent crime, reduce the fear of crime, apprehend those involved in criminal activity, and improve a community's quality of life.*
>
> (Morash and Ford, 2002, cited in Police Foundation, 2015, p 9)

Community policing has existed in some guise since as early as the 1960s, when unit beat policing in patrol cars was introduced with officers designated to certain neighbourhood areas. Chief constable, John Alderson, played a crucial role in the early development of community policing. Alderson argued that the introduction of unit beat patrols and 999 calls had led to a distance between the police and the public; therefore, he proposed the use of community policing methods which acknowledged the inability of the police to solve all crime while recognising the benefits of partnership working with local citizens and community organisations to construct a shared sense of community (Innes et al, 2020).

It was not until the Scarman report in 1981 that the negative consequences arising from oppressive policing tactics and lack of community consultation and engagement were highlighted. This prompted a shift away from crime control policing methods towards policing efforts which focused upon establishing relationships with local communities through a variety of different methods.

In 2003, the Home Office introduced the National Reassurance Policing Programme (NRPP), which sought to form an evidence base for reassurance policing as an effective method of crime reduction. The need for reassurance policing arose in response to a rising gap between what the public perceived to be rising crime rates, and the British Crime Survey 2005/2006 showing a decrease in recorded crime. With widespread public perceptions that crime rates were rising, fear of crime among the public remained high. Therefore, the NRPP sought to introduce various initiatives premised upon the idea that certain crimes and types of disorder have a disproportionate effect upon perceptions of safety and security and therefore should be prioritised (Innes et al, 2020).

Three key focus areas included:

1. a visible police presence would increase public confidence and therefore would improve public reassurance and reduce levels of fear of crime;

2. increased informal social control as locals took greater ownership of their area, which could serve to reduce crime and disorder;

3. working alongside community partners to reassure local communities and build bridges between the police and the public.

Following several pilot projects and trials, several valuable lessons were learnt about the circumstances in which reassurance policing was most effective.

> ## EVIDENCE-BASED POLICING
>
> In a study reported by Innes et al (2020), two homicides occurred in two areas which led to an increased police presence. In one area, the increased police presence was accompanied by a communications campaign which explained that they were there due to the homicide, and this was accepted by most community members. The second area engaged in no such communications, which led to community members being more sceptical of what the increased police presence signalled.
>
> From an early stage, it became evident that an increased police presence alone does not necessarily provide the public with reassurance and such efforts should be best coupled with proactive community engagement.

In seeking to engage with communities, however, the NRPP also highlighted another issue: it tended to be the same community members who were willing to engage with the police and these were often those who already perceived the police as legitimate.

Following various trials which reported that the reassurance model of community policing was capable of being successful in certain circumstances, these strategies were adopted more broadly across England and Wales and were renamed 'neighbourhood policing'. All neighbourhoods were to be assigned a local neighbourhood policing team, and in 2005 a national implementation programme was introduced. While crime reduction remained the aim of neighbourhood policing, a more flexible approach was adopted to ensure that neighbourhood policing was as responsive to community needs as possible. However, as no definition was provided for the term 'neighbourhood', this led to significant variations in the geographical area considered to be a neighbourhood across different police forces.

THE INTRODUCTION OF NEIGHBOURHOOD POLICING

In 2008, the Labour government rolled out their plans for neighbourhood policing. Each neighbourhood area was to have their own neighbourhood policing team with dedicated ring-fenced funding. Neighbourhood policing teams mainly included Police Community Support Officers (PCSOs), as explored below, and special constables, but were supported by police constables and a dedicated sergeant, in addition to partners from the local authority. Figure 1.1 shows how the government described the four aims of neighbourhood policing.

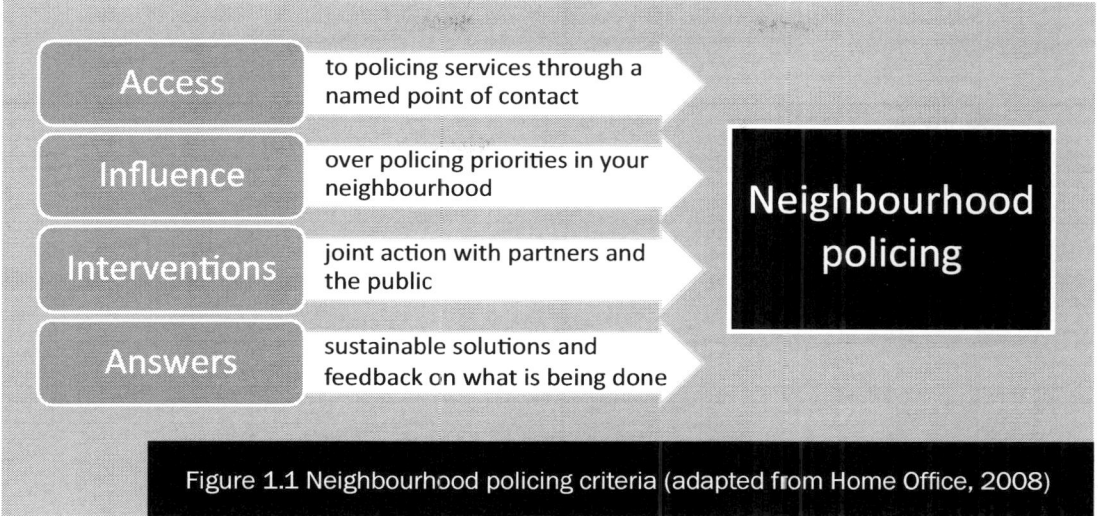

Figure 1.1 Neighbourhood policing criteria (adapted from Home Office, 2008)

Additional advice was also provided on 'critical success factors' which would assist in the effective '*development, implementation and integration of neighbourhood policing*' (Police Foundation, 2015, p 12). This included:

- ensuring efforts were supported by an overarching organisational strategy which incorporated neighbourhood policing;

- deployments were evidence-based to ensure the most effective approaches were adopted;

- dedicated teams were provided to support efforts, which was particularly important given that the model relied upon relationships of mutual trust;

- the identification of public priorities and adopting a collaborative approach to problem solving.

By 2008, Her Majesty's Inspectorate for Constabulary (HMIC, now HMICFRS) reported that all forces had managed to integrate a basic standard of neighbourhood policing into their forces, although room for improvement and development remained (HMICFRS). This included the need to better define geographical boundaries, inconsistencies between forces in terms of activities undertaken, engagement with communities, and the use of community intelligence. Further guidance was issued to forces to help ensure that neighbourhood policing could become a 'core' activity for all forces while recognising that this would require the model to be flexible enough to adapt to the unique needs of each neighbourhood.

6 POLICE PROBLEM-SOLVING MODELS AND THEORIES

A 'citizen-focused' approach based upon the following six principles was recommended (Mastrofski, 1999):

1. attentiveness;
2. reliability;
3. responsiveness;
4. competence;
5. manners;
6. fairness.

REFLECTIVE PRACTICE 1.1

LEVELS 4-6

Think about a time where you have displayed the above characteristics either at work, during volunteering or when socially interacting with others.

- How did you display these attributes?

- How was this received by the other individual(s) in the conversation?

- What influence do you think this had on your interaction with them?

- Are there any skills which you have yet to develop? If so, think about activities you could become involved with which would help you build these skills.

MODELS OF NEIGHBOURHOOD POLICING

There are five key models of neighbourhood policing, all of which are discussed throughout this book. Neighbourhood policing seeks to develop a comprehensive understanding of local issues with the intention of providing a tailored response, which may include adopting one or more of the models below depending on the crime issues.

1. INTENSIVE ENFORCEMENT

Intensive enforcement includes broken windows or zero-tolerance policing styles. Zero-tolerance policing prioritises aggressive order maintenance for low-level offences as a means of deterrence. It is premised on the idea that there is no acceptable level of crime and disorder and to accept even a low level would lead to a 'slippery slope' of more serious crime and disorder being conducted. However, this approach has been criticised for failing to address the underlying causes of crime. It is also most often used disproportionately against ethnic minorities and vulnerable community groups.

Broken Windows Theory suggests that ignoring low-level crime and disorder can increase fear within the area, which encourages more crime-fearing residents to leave. This leaves citizens who cannot afford to move, or who are party to the low-level crime and disorder, remaining in the area. This leads to less informal enforcement of social control and therefore the area becomes more attractive to other offenders (Wilson and Kelling, 1982). Neighbourhood policing can be used to address low-level issues of crime and disorder to ensure these issues are 'nipped in the bud', thereby preventing the escalation of more serious crimes.

2. HOT SPOT POLICING

Hot spot policing involves the targeting of resources in micro-areas where crime is most concentrated within a neighbourhood (see Chapter 2 for an in-depth explanation of hot spot policing). There is evidence to suggest that hot spot policing can be effective at crime reduction and as a deterrent (Sherman et al, 1989a); however, this varies according to the approaches and tactics used. In the context of neighbourhood policing, you need to have an open mind and accept that the approach adopted for one hot spot may be completely different to that required in another hot spot, despite them being in the same neighbourhood. Hot spots are most effective when combined with other strategies and not just patrols (Braga et al, 2012); therefore, in addition to conducting foot patrols, officers and PCSOs should actively be engaged in other interventions while based at the hot spot location.

3. PREDICTIVE POLICING

Predictive policing developed from the hot spot policing model. It is based upon the idea of 'repeat victimisation' and that individuals who have been victim to an offence are more likely to become a victim again in the future. Predictive policing adopts a data-led approach, using existing data to predict and prevent repeat victimisation and future offending in high-crime neighbourhoods. This provides numerous opportunities for you as neighbourhood officers to target interventions by identifying areas where car thefts have occurred and targeting your interventions towards those areas. The aim is to prevent the same vehicles, or other vehicles in that area, from being targeted.

4. PROBLEM-ORIENTED POLICING

Problem-oriented policing (POP) is a proactive model which also builds on the hot spot policing model; however, it focuses on addressing the root cause of recurring problems through a systematic, rigorous and multi-agency approach. When relying upon POP in a neighbourhood context, you will be seeking to establish why certain crimes and types of disorder occur and why previous approaches to address these issues have been unsuccessful. The SARA model is used in the planning and implementing of POP strategies and interventions, and this is discussed later in the chapter. Where properly implemented, POP initiatives can be highly successful in crime reduction (Weisburd et al, 2010). However, the success of the model largely depends on the robustness of the planning and analysis of the intervention, as well as a willingness to reflect upon the process and learn from previous iterations.

5. COLLECTIVE EFFICACY

Collective efficacy is a social process of informal control and social cohesion whereby neighbourhood residents collectively safeguard their area and are willing to intervene in potential crime and disorder in the interests of the collective good. While there is a lack of research in this area, some studies have indicated that even in high-crime-area hot spots, where there is a greater sense of collective efficacy among citizens, this may deter potential offenders (Bottoms, 2012).

THE IMPACT OF AUSTERITY

The introduction of austerity measures in 2010 resulted in extensive reductions in resources and frontline officers. This had a detrimental impact on neighbourhood policing as many neighbourhood policing teams were disbanded with remaining neighbourhood officers being removed from their community-based role and being redeployed to the frontline. For officers to be able to make long-term investments in improving communities, they require dedicated time to work with communities and implement and assess their interventions. Furthermore, austerity also had an impact on the issues which local communities faced (for example, crimes increasingly being committed online), which meant that some forces were no longer adequately equipped to address local policing demands.

CRITICAL THINKING ACTIVITY 1.1

LEVELS 4 AND 5

Can you think of three examples of how the lack of dedicated neighbourhood officers could negatively impact public confidence in policing?

LEVEL 6

Think about how austerity and the reduction in neighbourhood policing teams and officers may have had a detrimental impact upon public perceptions of legitimacy. What long-term consequences could this have for the police and the public?

Sample answers are provided at the end of this book.

Due to the increased demands of austerity, neighbourhood teams have increased their reliance upon targeted crime reduction and deterrence models, such as hot spot policing and predictive policing, as these allow the police to maximise existing resources. However, as stated by the Police Foundation (2015, p 25):

> *the effective deployment of resources in advance is heavily dependent on the quality of the predictive data and given its infancy (and its use so far with just a limited number of crimes), more research is needed before its utility is firmly endorsed.*

Similar budget cuts to other public sector organisations also led to difficulties in partnership working as some public sector organisations were either unable to help or increased the threshold at which they would help. This led to officers needing to either leave certain problems unresolved or attempt to assist with problems which were not traditionally within the remit of policing (College of Policing, 2018).

POLICE COMMUNITY SUPPORT OFFICERS

PCSOs are integral to the neighbourhood policing approach. The Police Reform Act 2002 created the role of PCSOs as dedicated community-based officers who would provide a visible presence in neighbourhoods. PCSOs would work within the local community to conduct uniformed patrols on foot or bike and engage with citizens to provide reassurance to local communities that the police care about crime issues in their area. Citizen surveys consistently indicate a strong preference for greater foot patrols (College of Policing, 2018).

Citizens who perceived the police as having a highly visible presence were found to be more likely to report higher satisfaction rates with the police, while citizens who reported rarely seeing an officer on patrol were much less likely to be satisfied (Police Foundation, 2015).

As most of their time is dedicated to foot patrols, PCSOs build an in-depth understanding of their local area and the individuals within that area, which is not only beneficial for building citizen trust over a longer period but also serves a vital intelligence-gathering function for the police. They also play a role in reducing low-level crime and disorder. Unfortunately, as much of this work cannot be quantified, this makes it difficult to understand the true impact of PCSOs as part of neighbourhood policing.

As PCSOs mainly fulfil a deterrent and community function, they do not have the same enforcement powers as officers as these were not deemed necessary. Consequently, some communities failed to accept PCSOs, perceiving them as inadequate and not engaged in 'real' police work (De Camargo, 2020). On the contrary, some evidence has been gathered to suggest that PCSOs are seen as valuable by local communities (Merritt, 2010). Research suggests that PCSOs are perceived as more 'approachable' and 'less threatening' than police constables, which leads to higher levels of public trust and confidence in the police (O'Neill, 2014).

CRITICAL THINKING ACTIVITY 1.2

LEVELS 4-6

Why might PCSOs be able to engage with communities better than regular police constables? Can you think of any perceived advantages for communities in communicating with an officer who does not have a power of arrest?

Sample answers are provided at the end of this book.

However, as a consequence of austerity, as non-warranted officers, many PCSOs were made redundant, which posed significant problems for neighbourhood policing (O'Neill, 2014). Some issues encountered included:

- relationships with communities which had been nurtured over years were lost;

- local citizens no longer had a dedicated individual they could contact;

- frontline officers no longer had time to conduct proactive foot patrols;

- police station closures led to some neighbourhood officers being moved to other locations;

- pressures on the frontline of reduced officers but increased demands due to similar budget cuts across all public services meant that officers had to prioritise urgent calls for service;

- loss of intelligence which was previously gathered by neighbourhood policing teams and PCSOs;

- loss of public confidence in the police and lower perceptions of legitimacy as local communities felt the police no longer care about their local area;

- lack of police constables available to support PCSOs where they have been retained but require back-up;

- increased time spent on response and without dedicated time assigned to neighbourhood functions; this can create an unpredictable workload for officers (Higgins, 2017).

THE IMPLEMENTATION OF NEIGHBOURHOOD POLICING

There are three vital aspects of neighbourhood policing (College of Policing, 2023a):

1. engaging communities;
2. problem solving;
3. targeting activity.

ENGAGING COMMUNITIES

A systematic review of studies examining neighbourhood policing was conducted by Gill et al (2014), which provides a comprehensive overview of the evidence base in this field. A summary is provided in Table 1.1.

Table 1.1 Engaging communities: evidence, research, advice

Evidence	Research	Advice
Effectiveness of community engagement		
Collaborating with the public on problem solving can reduce perceived disorder and increase public trust and legitimacy. Community engagement has a positive impact on crime and perceptions of anti-social behaviour and disorder.	(Myhill, 2012; Gill et al, 2014)	A targeted visible presence needs to be maintained over time.
Targeted foot patrols and community engagement leads to long-term decreases in criminal victimisation and disorder, increased perceptions of safety and trust in the police.	(Tuffin et al, 2006)	You should target patrols to hot spot locations, areas where police confidence is low and areas with high footfall. Optimise your time in hot spot locations.
Foot patrols alone are unlikely to increase public trust without community engagement, problem solving and perceived police fairness.	(Quinton and Morris, 2008)	While patrolling you should develop networks with communities, find out about local crime and disorder problems and have informal conversations. This can all support intelligence gathering.
Beat meetings alone are unlikely to effect change. However, events aimed at reaching a broad section of the community are more effective.	(Tuffin et al, 2006)	You should try to identify key places for different communities where you might find it easier to engage them, such as youth clubs, local transport bases, shops, places of worship etc.
		Use a range of different methods such as surveys, social media, door knocking etc. In particular, these should be aimed at where demand is high or public confidence is low, as well as areas of high footfall.
Implementation		
Flexible approach is required which reflects the needs of local communities.	(Myhill, 2012)	Clarify the purpose of engagement, for example, are you seeking to build trust in the aftermath of a critical incident, are you seeking to listen to communities to identify their needs etc?

Table 1.1 (continued)

Evidence	Research	Advice
Communities are not only geographically defined but can be communities of interest.	(Myhill, 2012)	Communities may be defined by people's interests, lifestyle, activities, age etc. It is particularly important to develop engagement strategies which seek to include vulnerable and hard-to-reach communities who may initially be reluctant to interact with the police.
Community engagement methods need to be periodically refreshed or communities begin to disengage.	(Skogan and Steiner, 2004)	Try a range of different locations, methods and times. Can you use social media? Try a range of approaches – invite community contributions for creative ideas and an increased sense of co-production.
Engagement should be representative of the local community and include people from marginalised groups by addressing barriers to engagement, such as language, gender, historical mistrust etc.	(Lister et al, 2015)	Identify barriers to engagement and try to work with the community and organisations to overcome them. This could include greater informal engagement, attending community spaces for engagement, using procedural justice, awareness raising through social media and trying to deal with long-standing community concerns. You should also consider a variety of methods which may work best for different communities, for example, interactive social media posts for youths, using the services of a translator if an area has a particularly high proportion of residents who have a first language which is not English etc.
Communities should be included within the engagement process, and it should become a two-way dialogue.	(Myhill, 2012)	How can you encourage communities to take ownership of solving local problems? Can you include them in the process of identifying and addressing crime issues? How can you support communities to take ownership and implement sustainable changes, for example, can you participate in problem-solving initiatives, can you set up a Neighbourhood Watch or Street Watch scheme?

Table 1.1 (continued)

Evidence	Research	Advice
Draw on existing networks of community groups. Mapping exercises can help officers understand local community stakeholders and existing groups they can tap into.	(Bullock and Leeney, 2013; Simmonds, 2015)	Community mapping can help tailor your engagement. You will need to establish different community groups, which ones are already engaged with the police, what type of engagement they want and barriers to such engagement. Reaching out to key individuals in the community may help you build these relations within the community. How can you make the most of existing opportunities for engagement?
The police need to keep locals informed of how to contact neighbourhood policing teams, neighbourhood priorities, actions taken by the police and how they can become involved.	(Bradford et al, 2009; Quinton, 2011).	Think about the costs associated with print and try to focus on specific areas where leaflets need to be distributed. Where else can you display important information? Community hubs and areas with a high footfall? Can you use social media instead?

Adapted from College of Policing (2018): *Neighbourhood Policing: Impact and Implementation*, and the *Neighbourhood Policing Guidelines* (2019).

CO-PRODUCTION AND COLLECTIVE EFFICACY

Section 34 of the Police Reform and Social Responsibility Act 2011 places an obligation upon forces to obtain public views on crime and disorder in their neighbourhood and to hold regular public meetings to encourage community consultation and co-operation. These are often referred to as 'beat meetings'. However, these meetings often only require consultation without a corresponding obligation upon forces to take action and without any means of citizens holding the police to account for their action (or lack of). For community input to be most effective, citizens need to be involved in decision making or empowered to take ownership of their neighbourhoods alongside more formal forms of social control and intervention offered by the police.

As established by the NRPP, the co-production of social control is important in community policing. Innes (2014) describes co-production as requiring *'individuals or groups from different backgrounds to share the work of: co-defining a problem; co-designing a solution and, co-delivering this response'* (as cited in Innes et al, 2020, p 45). Co-production seeks to redress the unequal balance of power encountered by citizens and empowers citizens to play an active role in the community. This can also lead to greater community cohesion and can strengthen collective efficacy.

As seen through this chapter, many initiatives proposed require neighbours to take some ownership of their micro-areas and intervene to safeguard their own areas. This trust can be built by raising familiarity between neighbours through opportunities for communication and while this is often undertaken independently by the residents, you can support this process through encouraging members to join or form a Neighbourhood Watch scheme. You can find out more about the Neighbourhood Watch scheme and the crime prevention advice and support they offer by following this link: www.ourwatch.org.uk.

CRITICAL THINKING ACTIVITY 1.3

LEVELS 4 AND 5

West Midlands Police has a 'Street Watch' scheme whereby local residents volunteer to accompany officers (often PCSOs) on patrols in their area while wearing high-visibility jackets to act as a local deterrent. Although these citizens have no formal policing powers, what do you think the benefits of them taking part in such an activity may be for the volunteers, the wider community and the police?

LEVEL 6

The area you are based in has had a series of burglaries and during a Neighbourhood Watch meeting residents have asked if you can attend and share advice on how to help keep their neighbourhood safe. What advice can you give them to help them protect their own neighbourhood and develop a stronger sense of social cohesion?

Sample answers are provided at the end of this book.

DEFINING PRIORITIES

In identifying community issues and identifying priorities, Tuffin et al (2006) identified a four-stage process, shown in Figure 1.2, which led to community engagement being more focused.

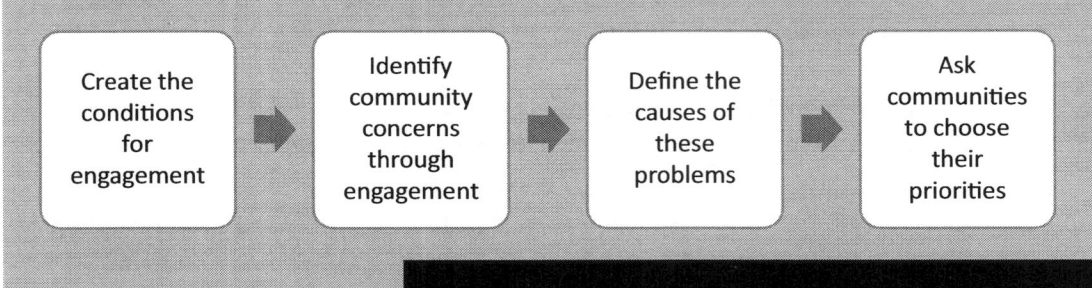

Figure 1.2 Four-stage community engagement process

CRITICAL THINKING ACTIVITY 1.4

LEVELS 4, 5 AND 6

You are asked to devise a survey for distribution around a local neighbourhood for the purpose of establishing what residents perceive to be local crime problems. Think of five survey questions you could ask to find this out.

LEVEL 6

You have completed the above activity. Your community has identified a shortlist of ten key problems in the local community. How will you decide which to prioritise? Think critically about the positives and negatives of each of the following options:

1. Issuing another survey asking people to shortlist again and rank their top five choices in order of priority.

2. Creating a social media poll asking people to vote.

3. Sharing the list with a neighbourhood panel and letting them decide on behalf of the local community.

Sample answers are provided at the end of this book.

However, over time, community priorities have become increasingly less dictated by the concerns of locals within neighbourhoods, and more focused upon higher harm and vulnerability concerns which may be less visible among communities. As Higgins notes in a report for the Police Foundation (2018, p 4): '*neighbourhood policing has become more ambiguous and multifaceted*'. Threats, risk, harm and vulnerability concerns play a bigger role in allocating community resources, despite these not always being an immediate or significant priority for local communities.

PROCEDURAL JUSTICE MODEL

How neighbourhood policing is delivered has considerable implications for public perceptions of fairness and police legitimacy. Therefore, it is important to highlight the benefits of adopting a procedurally just approach when interacting with citizens. This can strengthen perceptions of legitimacy and can lead to greater compliance by citizens to co-operate with the police and not break the law (Tyler, 2004). In the context of neighbourhood policing, you should aim to increase the quality of everyday contact with citizens. Adopting the procedural justice model can help to ensure that your interactions are perceived as fair, just and legitimate.

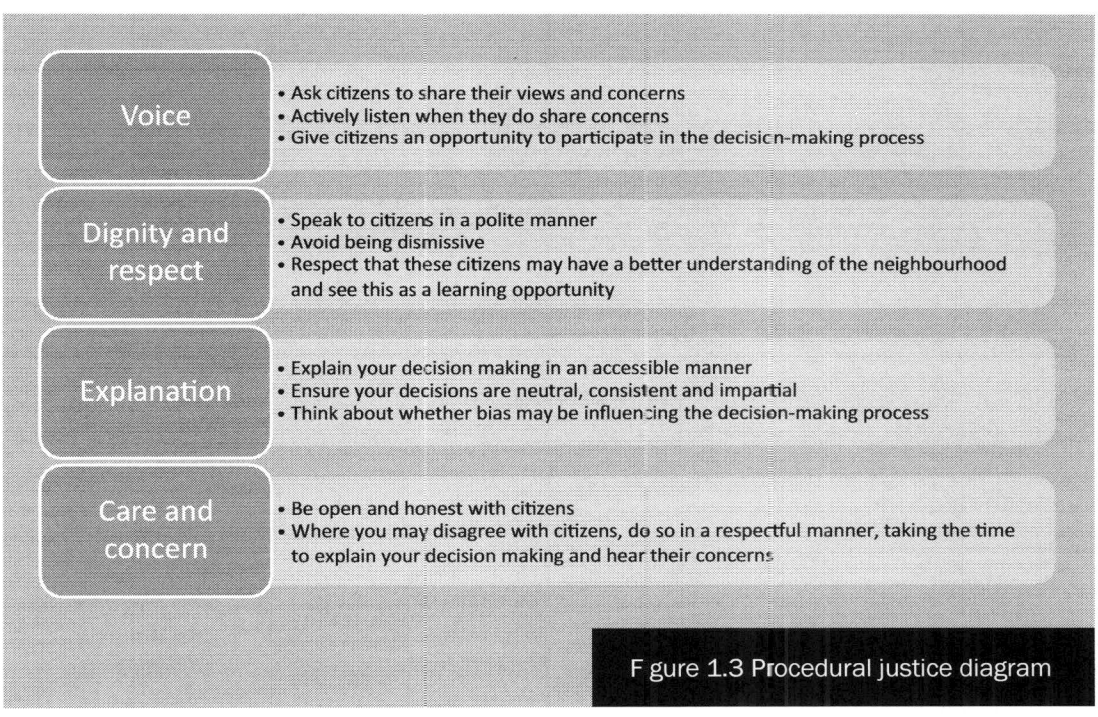

Figure 1.3 Procedural justice diagram

PROBLEM SOLVING

The problem-solving strategy is one of the most effective for reducing crime, disorder and demand. To guide you through the problem-solving strategy, we use the SARA model, which is further explored in Chapter 2.

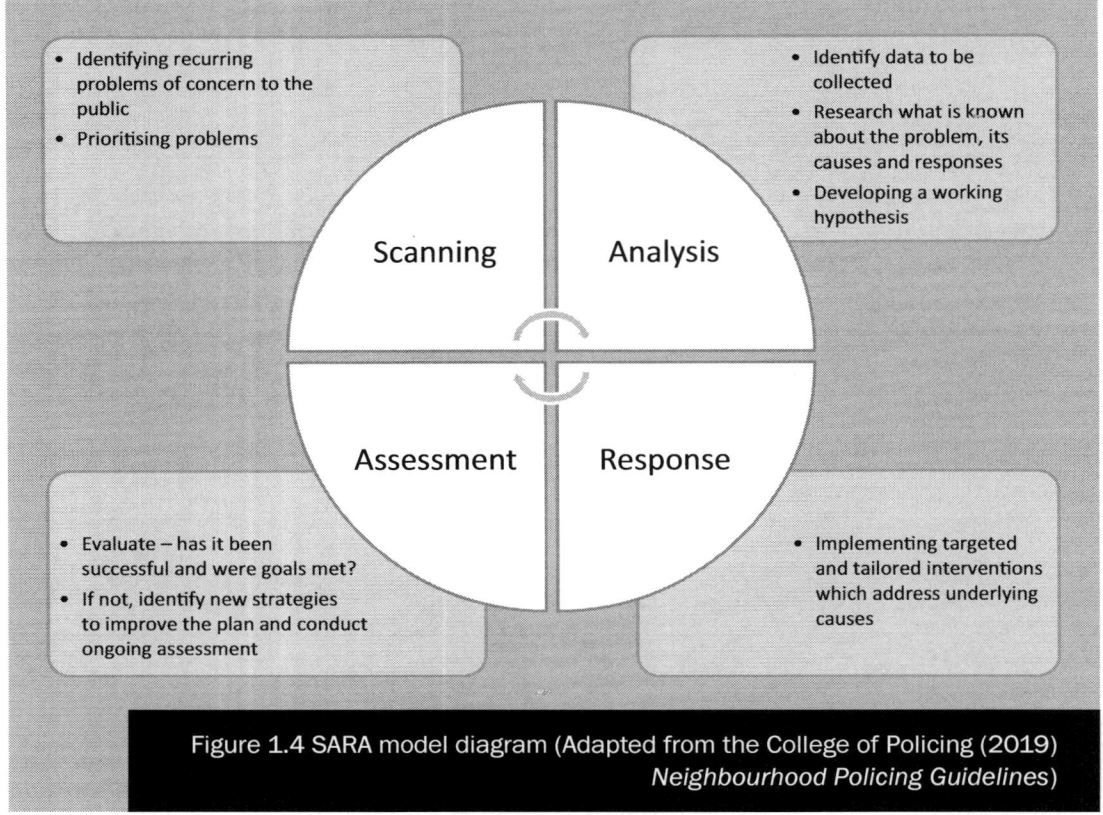

Figure 1.4 SARA model diagram (Adapted from the College of Policing (2019) *Neighbourhood Policing Guidelines*)

IMPLEMENTING THE SARA MODEL

Crime and disorder can be reduced by using a variety of structured problem-solving processes to understand the root causes of local crime issues (Weisburd et al, 2010).

SCANNING

Scanning can be police and partner-led or community-led. The police and partner-led approach examines data from multiple sources to identify patterns indicative of demand. Problem solving in hot spots is more effective at reducing crime in hot spots than simply an increased police presence. It also has a longer-term impact (Braga et al, 2012). What data can you draw on to identify hot spots? Can the data also help you identify areas where people are most vulnerable to harm? Can you identify the people most likely to cause harm? Don't forget that hot spots may not be effective for less visible crimes such as cybercrime; therefore, you may need to adopt an alternative approach.

A community-led approach includes asking communities to indicate which crimes have the biggest effect on them. These may be issues which are considered low harm and therefore may not necessarily be policing problems. Research indicates that best practice is to include the public in identifying and defining the problem, as well as in awareness-raising initiatives (Skogan and Steiner, 2004; Quinton and Morris, 2008). Where there is some conflict between the community-led approach and policing and partner-led approach, you may need to take the following actions:

- deciding which problems to prioritise;

- deciding who is best to address certain problems.

ANALYSIS

Analysis requires a detailed problem specification that should be created based upon multiple sources of information to create a tailored solution (Tuffin et al, 2006). This can be drawn from multi-agency or community partners, or you can also draw upon the support of analytical specialists for a more thorough analysis of the data.

An example for burglaries could include:

- geographical maps showing exactly which houses on the roads were targeted;

- graphs and bar charts showing the type of property and the point and method of entry;

- tables showing the frequency at which houses/streets were targeted;

- tables tracking the interventions and current burglary rates with space for future rates to be measured and entered.

EVIDENCE-BASED POLICING

A study by Turley et al (2012) examined six different areas and the partnership between the police and other agencies in implementing neighbourhood policing initiatives. Each site had a dedicated police neighbourhood manager who oversaw the implementation, planning, delivery and review of the services and who would liaise with other partner agencies and the wider community. This led to citizens and practitioners feeling more aware and empowered, while perceiving that crime had reduced. Some sites identified a key location where the police and partner agencies could work together to facilitate discussions and planning, and to encourage the sharing of data and intelligence. However, where citizens were less trusting of the police, this had a negative impact on their perception of the partner agencies too. The study also highlighted the importance of the neighbourhood manager extending their reach to the wider community, including harder-to-reach groups.

You should try and ensure the data gathered is as precise as possible. The problem analysis triangle provides a method for you to think through recurring crime and disorder issues. It assumes that crime occurs when there is a motivated offender, a suitable target and a place without a capable guardian, and by removing an aspect of the triangle you can minimise opportunities for crime to occur. The College of Policing advises that this should cover at least two aspects of the problem analysis triangle in forming a problem specification (College of Policing, 2019).

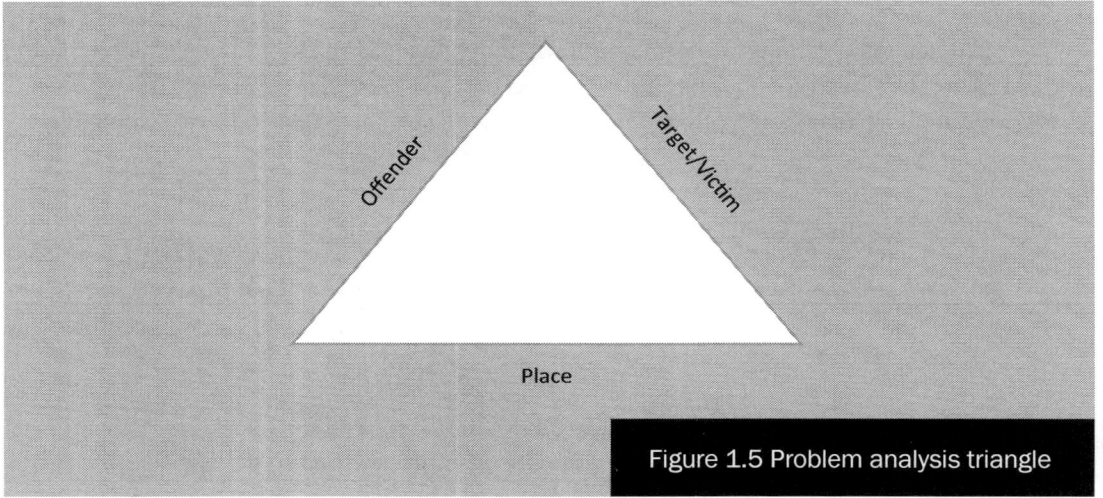

Figure 1.5 Problem analysis triangle

RESPONSE

Response includes identifying appropriate responses to the problems identified in the previous steps and deciding who is best placed to address those issues. Partnership working is essential. Where priorities are aligned with partners, this can increase co-operation and capacity and reduce duplication (Skogan and Steiner, 2004). This may also encourage partners to take ownership of certain problems themselves, which may be beneficial for reducing demands on the police and increasing a sense of community cohesion. For example, issues with dog fouling should be dealt with by the local authority and issues regarding adverse childhood experiences are better responded to by schools and health services.

It is important to remember that not all interventions will be able to address the root cause of the issues and therefore it may also be beneficial to consider implementing more preventative measures such as situational crime prevention strategies (see Chapter 5) or support from more preventative units such as the Violence Reduction Partnership or other early or community-based interventions.

In exploring potential interventions which may be suitable for your area, you could research ideas on what has been implemented in other areas and forces.

CRITICAL THINKING ACTIVITY 1.5

The 'crime reduction toolkit' allows you to search for evidence-based approaches to crime reduction. It allows you to search by the desired effect you are seeking (diversion, prevention or reoffending), the offence and population and any specific factors such as alcohol or drugs.

LEVELS 4 AND 5

Familiarise yourself with the crime reduction toolkit at: www.college.police.uk/research/crime-reduction-toolkit. Have a read through some of the studies which have been conducted and how the responses implemented vary.

LEVEL 6

Choose two studies for the same offence and compare the approach of both. What are their strengths and weaknesses? How could they have been improved?

Assessment is an important stage in problem solving which requires regular monitoring and an impact assessment. The absence of this can be a barrier to evaluating effectiveness and informing future problem-solving activities (Bullock and Tilley, 2003). Without robust monitoring mechanisms it may not be clear whether your intervention was successful, where there may be room for improvement and whether any adjustments are needed. The use of a comparison group can also be useful for confidently assessing the effects of the intervention. Randomised control trials are a rigorous and effective method for doing so.

Good interventions should:

- have clear and measurable objectives;

- gather quantitative data which allow for trends/progress to be identified and will facilitate the measurement of specific impact and outcomes;

- report in an open and honest manner;

- be realistic about what can be achieved with the budget and resources available and calculate whether the intervention was cost-effective;

- include opportunities for ongoing reflective practice;

- gather qualitative data, particularly from local community members and victims as to their feedback;

- include a measure of their longevity and sustainability, together with the ability to repeat the intervention;

- identify challenges and barriers to intervention;

- assess wider considerations such as potential crime displacement or diffusion of benefits.

POLICING SPOTLIGHT

You are based in a local area and have met local community members to discuss local policing concerns. You asked the analysts to provide you with data on areas where crime is most concentrated. They advised that the bus station in town had numerous reports of anti-social behaviour and several students from Greenrow High School have been subject to muggings after school.

After a community meeting, citizens also report additional crimes. Some shopkeepers in a certain area reported an increase in low-level thefts between 2200 and 0130 from three corner shops which have no CCTV and the police have not been able to attend. Some community members also reported issues with littering in their local park. Another school, Cherry High, reported issues with students arriving very late to school because they are hanging around in a café at the top of the road the school is on.

CRITICAL THINKING ACTIVITY 1.6

Applying the SARA model, work your way through the following:

LEVELS 4–6

1. How would you decide which issues to prioritise?

2. How could you draw upon your partners and other organisations to help address these issues?

LEVEL 6

3. What solutions might you propose?

4. How will you evaluate their effectiveness?

Sample answers are provided at the end of this book.

TARGETING ACTIVITY

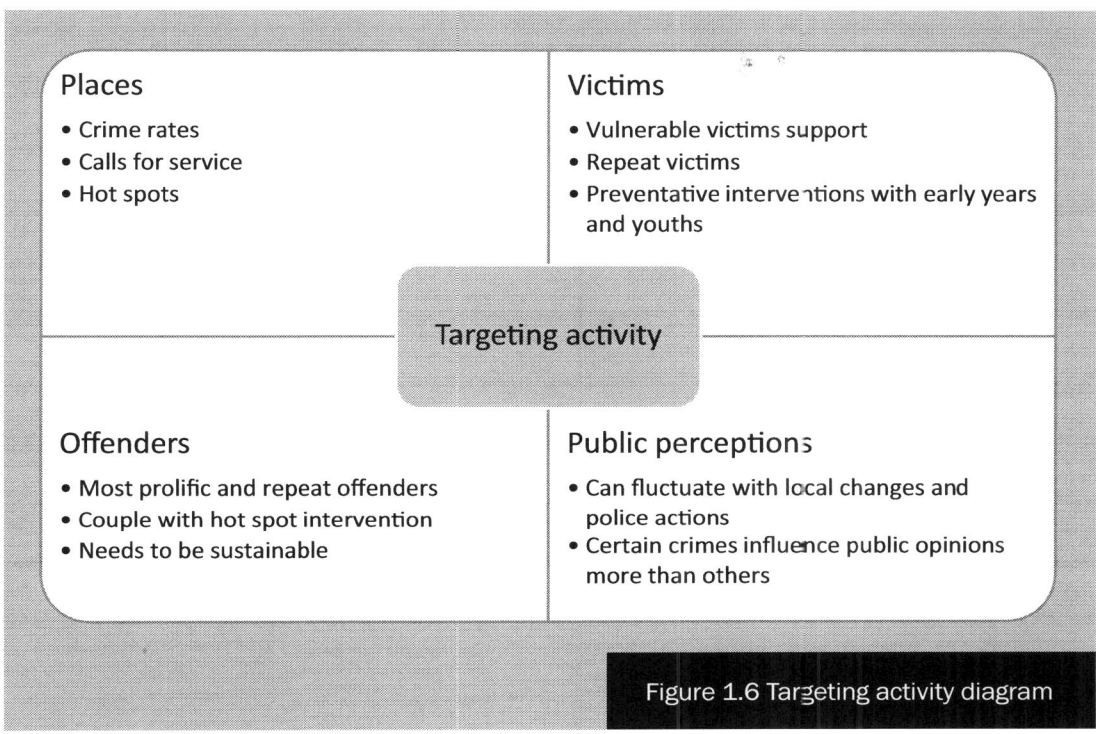

Figure 1.6 Targeting activity diagram

ETHICAL CONSIDERATIONS

Given the varied and diverse activities which occur under the neighbourhood policing model, the nature of the ethical issues encountered will often depend upon the initiatives employed to address the crime problems identified. One underlying concern remains the policing of diverse communities, particularly as the neighbourhood policing model relies heavily upon community co-operation.

For ethnic minority communities, youths or communities in high-crime areas, previous negative encounters with the police may prevent them from willingly engaging in neighbourhood policing initiatives. Greater reluctance may be experienced where tactics used involved intensive enforcement strategies such as zero-tolerance policing or increased stop and search in hot spot locations. These activities can undermine public confidence in the police where communities believe they are being unfairly targeted.

Maintaining an open line of communication, increased publicity surrounding the purpose of police presence in the area and adopting a procedurally just approach may assist you in mitigating these concerns to some extent. However, ensuring that you seek to engage these communities in a dialogue prior to more intensive enforcement activities is likely to be most effective in building perceptions of legitimacy and allowing community members to help shape policing responses in a manner which is acceptable to them. This is not only more likely to secure their co-operation, but can also encourage community-based organisations and community and faith leaders to support policing efforts in this respect. Where consultations are not fully representative of all communities, this can lead to some neighbourhood policing efforts being counterproductive and alienating some citizens.

THE FUTURE OF NEIGHBOURHOOD POLICING

While neighbourhood policing itself continues to remain a fundamental aspect of policing, the model is likely to encounter several challenges in contemporary and future society. As a result of austerity, financial downturns and fractured and divisive political and economic policies, neighbourhoods are becoming increasingly fragmented, with diverse populations and needs; therefore, it is becoming harder for policing to meet those challenges.

Social media is also likely to play an increasing role in the future of neighbourhood policing. Social media provides an alternative means of community engagement, which may be particularly effective in the aftermath of austerity and reduced resources. Social media provides a cost-effective way of connecting and engaging with communities, sharing information and inviting participation. Given the wide reach of social media, it may be more effective in reaching certain community groups, such as youths who may be reluctant to attend a physical meeting, or parents of young children who may be unable to attend evening meetings. You could also utilise social media for building networks with vital community partners and key figures.

REFLECTIVE PRACTICE 1.2

LEVELS 5 AND 6

Read the Policing Vision 2025. What emphasis is placed on neighbourhood policing in the future of policing? How do you see yourself engaging in neighbourhood policing in the future?

SUMMARY OF KEY CONCEPTS

This chapter has explored the following key concepts.

- Reassurance policing is the idea that a visible police presence, via officers conducting foot patrols, for example, reassures citizens that officers care about local crime issues and are available to deal with them, as well as actively addressing issues in those locations.

- Partnership working involves working with other organisations, whether they have a legal responsibility to support citizens, such as local authorities, or are community-based organisations who can support policing.

- Collective efficacy is the term given to the informal social control of an area by residents who feel a collective sense of responsibility for maintaining and protecting their area.

- PCSOs are officers who have a visible police presence in areas although they are not police constables and therefore do not have the full powers and responsibilities of police officers. Their role is to conduct foot patrols and gather information from actively engaging with communities.

CHECK YOUR KNOWLEDGE

1. Why was the neighbourhood policing model introduced?

2. What are the three key aspects of implementing neighbourhood policing models?

3. Describe three ways of successfully engaging with communities.

4. What does the SARA model require?

5. Why do PCSOs serve a vital function in neighbourhood policing?

6. How can hot spots be useful for targeting activity within a neighbourhood?

Sample answers are provided at the end of this book.

FURTHER READING

ARTICLES, BOOKS AND CHAPTERS

Fielding, N G (1995) *Community Policing*. Oxford: Oxford University Press.

Gill, C, Weisburd, D, Telep, C W, Vitter, Z and Bennett, T (2014) Community-Oriented Policing to Reduce Crime, Disorder and Fear of Increased Satisfaction and Legitimacy among Citizens: A Systematic Review. *Journal of Experimental Criminology*, 10(4): 399–428.

Innes, M, Roberts, C, Lowe, T and Innes, H (2020) *Neighbourhood Policing: The Rise and Fall of a Policing Model*. Oxford: Oxford University Press.

Quinton, P and Morris, J (2008) *Neighbourhood Policing: The Impact of Piloting and Early National Implementation*. London: Home Office.

Weisburd, D and Telep, C W (2014) Hot Spot Policing: What We Know and What We Need to Know. *Journal of Contemporary Criminal Justice*, 30(2): 200–20.

WEBSITES

College of Policing (2023) Neighbourhood policing. [online] Available at: www.college.police.uk/guidance/neighbourhood-policing (accessed 9 March 2023).

Interested in neighbourhood policing? Have a look at the recruitment page for more information.
Police (2023) Join the Police. [online] Available at: www.joiningthepolice.co.uk/training-progression/career-progression/role-spotlights/neighbourhood-policing (accessed 9 March 2023).

CHAPTER 2
HOT SPOT POLICING

LEARNING OBJECTIVES

AFTER READING THIS CHAPTER YOU WILL BE ABLE TO:

- understand the definition of hot spot policing;

- explore a range of policing activities used in hot spot policing strategies;

- analyse and understand existing research conducted into hot spot policing;

- evaluate how to effectively implement hot spot policing strategies;

- consider practical challenges, barriers and ethical considerations involved in hot spot policing strategies.

INTRODUCTION

Hot spot policing is a policing strategy which acknowledges that most crime occurs in micro-locations, and that by targeting police activities and resources to those specific locations, crime reduction efforts are more likely to be successful. There is a strong evidence base emerging for the effectiveness of hot spot locations (Braga et al, 2019) with an increasing number of forces adopting a hot spot policing approach. Over the past 25 years, research suggests that crime is not evenly distributed across urban areas; rather, it is concentrated in very small places, or 'hot spots', which generate half of all criminal events (Pierce et al, 1988; Sherman et al, 1989b).

This chapter begins by exploring the definition of hot spot policing and what the strategy entails. Next, it examines the theoretical basis for hot spot policing so you can understand the motivation behind forces adopting a more targeted approach to crime reduction. It explores the two main methods of hot spot policing: increased officer presence and the implementation of problem-oriented policing strategies. The chapter helps you understand how to target activities within hot spot locations, drawing upon the evidence base from existing studies. The final section of the chapter explores barriers and challenges to hot spot policing which you may encounter and provides suggestions on how these can be addressed and further considerations.

The Beating Crime Plan 2021 identifies hot spot policing as an essential part of crime reduction efforts, particularly in relation to serious violence, with dedicated funding being introduced by the Home Office to support hot spot policing efforts, particularly in large urban towns and cities. Therefore, it is likely that hot spot policing will become an increasingly relied-upon strategy during your career as an officer.

WHAT IS HOT SPOT POLICING?

Hot spot policing is a term given to the targeting of police activity and resources to specific geographical areas where crime is most heavily concentrated. 'Hot' indicates a high level of crime and 'spot' refers to the location. Hot spot policing is a proactive policing strategy, one which you may also have heard referred to as a 'place-based' policing strategy. Hot spot policing is premised upon the idea that crime is not evenly distributed: certain areas persistently experience more crime and disorder. By increasing policing activity within the specific areas where crime is most clustered, the police can reduce crime within that area.

Although there are no explicit limits on the geographical area of a hot spot, these are often micro-areas such as a specific street or group of streets, pubs and off-licence establishments, or bus stops (Braga and Weisburd, 2010). Just by standing in the middle of the hot spot, you should be able to see most it, which indicates how small the area should be (Sherman et al, 1989b).

Figure 2.1 Example of a violent crime hot spot map (adapted from Mapping London, 2013)

Traditionally, policing activity is primarily focused upon individuals, whereas the hot spot policing strategy focuses upon locations (Weisburd, 2008). The concentration of crime in a few hot spot places seems even greater when it is compared to the concentration of crime among individuals (Spelman and Eck, 1989). As such, the hot spot policing strategy is a catch-all term for any activities deployed within the hot spot location which were introduced for the purposes of crime prevention.

Activities may include:

- increased foot patrols by uniformed officers;

- increased presence of plain-clothed officers conducting observations;

- installation and active monitoring of CCTV;

- use of other forms of surveillance technology such as automatic number plate recognition (ANPR) cameras;

- problem-oriented policing strategies;

- increased use of police stops (including stop and search and vehicle stops);

- increased arrests (for example, as part of a crackdown on drugs);

- implementing situational crime prevention strategies;

- increased targeting or surveillance of known repeat offenders;

- increased community engagement and neighbourhood co-operation.

The policing activities you choose will be tailored to those which are most appropriate to the specific crime issue. Although targeting activity to a specific location is proven to have crime reduction benefits, the broad range of policing activities has meant that it is unclear which activities are most beneficial (Braga et al, 2019). Moreover, as explored in this chapter, the impact of hot spot policing is not yet fully understood, particularly in England and Wales, as most studies into hot spot policing have been conducted in the United States.

There is strong evidence to suggest that hot spot policing can be an effective means of crime prevention (Braga et al, 2012). The benefits of hot spot policing have been examined for a broad range of crimes including burglary and property offences, drugs possession and drug dealing, violent crime, as well as other forms of disorder. Systematic reviews of hot spot policing have been conducted which evaluate the extensive evidence base and facilitate a comparison of key findings across the studies. Many of these findings have been drawn upon in this chapter; however, Braga et al (2019) conducted a systematic review of 65 evaluations of hot spot policing studies, and it is recommended that you read this for a more in-depth understanding of the existing research which has been conducted in this field.

THEORETICAL FOUNDATIONS

The theoretical basis for hot spot policing arises from Deterrence Theory and Routine Activity Theory. Chapter 4 provides a more in-depth discussion of both approaches; therefore, only a brief explanation is provided in this section.

Deterrence Theory suggests that people make rational decisions as to whether the cost of committing a crime outweighs the benefits of committing the crime. Where punishment is certain, swiftly imposed and sufficiently severe, individuals are less likely to want to engage in committing crimes (Beetham, 1991). Therefore, if you can increase the likelihood of a suspect being caught, reduce the time it takes to catch them after the crime or increase the severity of the punishment, you can deter individuals from committing crime.

For example, if you were to increase the number of foot patrols conducted within a hot spot area, suspects are likely to associate increased officer presence with a greater likelihood of being caught. Your physical presence in the hot spot location would also reduce your response time to the incident, further strengthening the deterrent effect.

Routine Activity Theory (Cohen and Felson, 1979) is described in detail in Chapter 4; however, in brief, it refers to the idea that there are three necessary components for crime to be committed:

1. a likely offender;

2. a suitable target;

3. the absence of capable guardians in the area.

If you remove any of these three components, an area becomes more susceptible to crime and disorder. By implementing hot spot policing strategies such as increased foot patrols or increased CCTV surveillance, you provide a capable guardian to safeguard against the commission of further crimes.

THE DEVELOPMENT OF HOT SPOT POLICING STRATEGIES

THE IDENTIFICATION OF HOT SPOT LOCATIONS

The concept of officers becoming familiar with certain locations and thereby increasing their attention on those locations where crime is most prevalent is not new. However, officers do not always have an accurate gauge of specific areas where crime is most prevalent (Macbeth and Ariel, 2019). More data gathering and monitoring, as well as technological advancements, allow hot spot locations to be more accurately identified, which facilitates a more proactive and strategic approach to hot spot policing. Crime data gathered by forces can be used to create geographic information system (GIS) maps and crime mapping software which identify hot spot locations. These can be used to predict where crime may occur in the future, based on data from the past, and can therefore inform future deployment decisions.

A location does not need to have a set rate of crime before it is considered 'hot'. Instead, it will be seen as having high rates of crime relative to other specific locations at a given time. You are likely to receive data and information from specialist data analysts to help you identify potential hot spot locations. However, it should be noted that only recorded crime and public calls are taken into account; therefore, deployments to hot spot locations based upon this data may not fully represent the scale of crime and disorder experienced within an area.

CRITICAL THINKING ACTIVITY 2.1

LEVEL 4

Can you think of any sources from which data could be drawn to identify where crime occurs?

LEVELS 5 AND 6

Can think of other reasons why recorded crime data may lead to the inaccurate identification of hot spot locations?

Sample answers are provided at the end of this book.

Technological advancements have strengthened hot spot policing in many ways, including:

- being able to identify the 'hottest' hot spots including *where* the most crime occurs, and *when* it occurs;

- optimisation of officer deployments between patrols;

- linking of crime trends in hot spot locations to patrols;

- tracking the impact of police activity within the hot spot.

Given the micro-locations of hot spot policing, it is important that officers remain within that specific location. GPS software has been used to track whether officers remained within the hot spot location and for what duration. Tracking can also be achieved through force-issued mobile apps which allow officers to export data which can be used to map where an officer has patrolled and the duration of the patrol, among other factors.

EVIDENCE-BASED POLICING

In one of the few UK studies examining hot spot policing, Fielding and Jones (2012) used predictive policing data to create a colour-coded map showing risk categories associated with domestic burglary in Trafford, Manchester. This map was then used to identify hot spot locations where officers conducted increased foot patrols. To test the effect of the hot spot strategy, officers were split into two groups with the experimental group being deployed to the hot spot location. GPS technology was used to track where officers were patrolling. While a decrease in domestic burglaries was reported in both groups, the experimental group were the only ones to report a statistically significant reduction in burglaries.

HOT SPOT POLICING ACTIVITIES

This section explores activities which can be undertaken within a hot spot location. It draws upon the evidence base of existing studies examining the effect of hot spot policing. However, most of the research into hot spot policing has been conducted in the United States, which may limit the generalisability of some of these studies to policing in England and Wales.

In addition, there is also a lack of robust evidence as to the effectiveness of the different strategies adopted given the broad range of activities employed. There are two main categories to hot spot policing: increasing visible officer presence and problem-oriented policing (Braga et al, 2019).

INCREASING VISIBLE OFFICER PRESENCE

Preventative patrols is the term given to officers conducting directed foot patrols or vehicle patrols at hot spot locations. This approach is also known as 'high-visibility' policing. Often, in addition to simply patrolling, officers will also be seeking to engage in increased enforcement activity, including greater police stops and arrests, while conducting their patrols.

In a study published in 1995, Koper analysed 17,000 observations of police patrols in Minneapolis, USA, to identify the optimal time which officers should spend patrolling a hot spot location and how this impacted its deterrent effect. Koper identified that each additional minute officers spent patrolling a hot spot led to a 23 per cent increase in the time it took before crime occurred after the officers had left the hot spot location. This became known as the 'Koper Curve'. However, after 15 minutes, crime reduction efforts diminished.

These findings were echoed by a study in 2015 which examined the use of increased foot patrols across Birmingham, England and found that patrols between 10 and 15 minutes were the most effective and led to a 14 per cent reduction in street crimes and anti-social behaviour (Williams, 2015). Crime also decreased in areas surrounding the hot spot, suggesting that the intervention had positive diffusion effects (Williams and Coupe, 2017).

EVIDENCE-BASED POLICING

Essex Police conducted a trial whereby 20 of the 'hottest' hot spot locations for serious assaults, robbery and drug dealing were identified. Two officers would park in a visible location at the area and conduct a foot patrol within a small area of 150 m² once a day for 15–20 minutes.
Serious violence was reduced by 88.5 per cent on days when the patrols were conducted, and street offences reduced by 31 per cent, indicating that foot patrols can be a highly effective method in preventing serious violence in areas where such crimes are heavily concentrated (Basford et al, 2021).

When conducting foot patrols, you should proactively consider conducting foot patrols of up to 15 minutes in an unpredictable pattern between different hot spot locations; this would maximise the deterrent effect of the patrol as police presence could be expected at any time. As foot patrols only appear to have a short-term deterrent effect, they should be used in combination with other problem-solving approaches (Taylor et al, 2011).

CRIME DISPLACEMENT

A key critique of the hot spot policing concept is the risk of 'spatial crime displacement', that is, focusing on small geographical locations may lead to offenders simply moving to a surrounding area to commit crime (Braga and Weisburd, 2010). In practice, however, this does not appear to have been the case, with increased police activity in hot spot locations most often leading to a reduction in crime and disorder (Weisburd et al, 2006). In fact, hot spot policing has been shown to have a small diffusion effect into neighbouring areas, which suggests that the benefits of the hot spot policing approach are not only felt in the hot spot location but also in surrounding areas. This mitigates concerns around the displacement of crime.

CRITICAL THINKING ACTIVITY 2.2

LEVEL 4

Can you think of how austerity measures and reduced financial resources may impact the ability of police forces to conduct foot patrols?

LEVELS 5 AND 6

Evaluate the effectiveness of hot spot policing as a policing strategy. Is it a more short-term deterrent? Can it be repeated indefinitely? Or is it a long-term strategy which seeks to address the underlying causes of crime?

Sample answers are provided at the end of this book.

High-visibility policing is also associated with greater public confidence, and therefore is sometimes also termed 'reassurance policing' as it reassures citizens that the police are available to respond if an emergency were to occur and that the police are active within their communities conducting their duties. Targeted foot patrols have been found to improve public confidence and perceptions of safety, as well as reducing crime when implemented alongside other problem-solving and community engagement efforts (Tuffin et al, 2006).

OFFICER PERCEPTIONS

A study of officer perceptions of hot spot policing in the UK reported that officers were cynical of the strategy (Wain and Ariel, 2014). Many officers preferred to rely upon their own discretion in identifying the most problematic locations. However, research conducted by Wheeler and Reuter in the United States suggested that officers often over-estimated the size of the hot spot location which led to less efficient patrols (Wheeler and Reuter, 2021). Wheeler and Reuter (2021) also found that relying upon GIS maps to identify hot spots with more precision may be more beneficial.

An additional barrier to implementing a hot spot policing method may be a lack of motivation among officers to pursue crime prevention efforts. As argued by Ariel (2022), many officers primarily perceive their role as 'crime fighters' and the mundane tasks of increased patrols may not be motivating for some officers. Although officers could be provided with real-time feedback on the progress and effectiveness of the policing activity used at the time.

REFLECTIVE PRACTICE 2.1

LEVELS 4–6

You have been tasked with reducing vehicle thefts which are occurring on a specific road. Your sergeant has instructed you and your partner to conduct increased vehicle patrols in the area and to place leaflets on each car asking them to consider investing in a steering wheel lock or similar device. Your partner believes that sitting in the patrol car each evening is a waste of time and that no one reads leaflets anyway.

How do you think you would respond? Is there sufficient evidence to suggest targeted patrols deter offenders? How does educating citizens in keeping their possessions safe relate to Routine Activity Theory?

Sample answers are provided at the end of this book.

PROBLEM-ORIENTED POLICING

Problem-oriented policing (POP) was introduced by Goldstein (1979), who believed that policing was often too reactive and a more proactive approach in addressing underlying causes of crime would be more effective. The POP model is sometimes referred to as problem-solving policing and it allows for the development of targeted interventions aimed at reducing crime and disorder. As stated by Braga et al (2019), problem-oriented policing seeks to '*change the underlying conditions and situational dynamics that caused problems to recur in high-activity crime places*' (Braga et al, 2019, p 10). That is, it encourages officers to identify and target the underlying problems which cause crime by analysing specific recurrent crime issues of concern to communities. It often seeks to do so by increasing the risk associated with committing certain offences, increasing the effort required to commit the offence or reducing its attractiveness. The POP model formed the basis for the development of the SARA model of problem solving (Eck and Spelman, 1987).

In implementing problem-oriented policing, the SARA model of problem solving can be an effective tool.

- **S**can – identify and prioritise the most important problems.

- **A**nalyse – gather information or intelligence to help you understand the causes of the problem and accordingly design response strategies.

- **R**espond – implementation of bespoke solutions which address the underlying cause of the problem.

- **A**ssess – evaluate whether the responses have been successful. If not, repeat the model until effective solutions are found.

See the following link for more information on the SARA model: www.college.police.uk/guidance/problem-solving-policing.

While both hot spot policing and problem-oriented policing focus upon crime patterns in specific locations, there are differences between the two. When adopting a problem-oriented policing approach, your attention will be focused upon certain types of offences, for example a drugs crackdown within a certain area known for drug dealing. However, a hot spot policing approach is led by identification of the area as being one in which crime occurs. As such, problem-oriented policing can be an effective tool for use within hot spot areas.

A study found that a problem-oriented policing approach to hot spots was twice as effective as increased foot patrols (Braga et al, 2012). Although the benefits of a problem-oriented policing approach were not immediately evident, they produced a longer-lasting effect.

POLICING SPOTLIGHT

This scenario is typical of one which may require problem-solving strategies. Broad Street is a road in Birmingham which has a strong night-time economy. A few nightclubs are experiencing an increase in drug dealing outside their premises after closing time. About 200 people leave the clubs between the hours of 3am to 4am, which has made it difficult for the four security personnel at those clubs to monitor the crowds. In addition, a handful of citizens are becoming disorderly and refusing to leave.

CRITICAL THINKING ACTIVITY 2.3

LEVELS 4-6

Evaluate the potential effectiveness of the following problem-solving strategies at the hot spot, drawing upon the SARA model.

- Advising the nightclubs to increase CCTV coverage to include the outside area.

- Increased officer foot patrols through the night.

- Requesting officers with drugs dogs to stand near the hot spot between 3am and 4am.

- Asking the nightclubs to increase the number of security personnel they employ until the problem begins to reduce.

LEVEL 6

Can you think of any other problem-solving strategies which could be implemented to help address these issues?

Sample answers are provided at the end of this book.

Problem-oriented policing strategies can include the adoption of zero-tolerance policing strategies and other intense forms of law enforcement which often include more abrasive techniques such as 'broken windows' style crackdowns. Broken Windows Theory (explored in more detail in Chapter 5) suggests that where the police and residents ignore visible low-level disorder within a location, this increases fear and withdrawal by residents of that location, which leads to less informal enforcement of social control and therefore allows more serious crimes to be committed (Wilson and Kelling, 1982).

It has been argued that this type of police enforcement may be counterproductive. Firstly, there is a risk that, particularly in residential areas or community spaces, increased officer presence may lead to citizens wrongly perceiving that crime has increased within those areas which make citizens more fearful (Weisburd et al, 2010).

Secondly, where policing styles are more abrasive, this can reduce citizens' perception of police legitimacy. If citizens believe that the disproportionate attention they are receiving because of hot spot policing strategies is unfair or unequally distributed, this may have a negative impact on the way they perceive the police as legitimate. Rosenbaum (2006) argues that this may lead to citizens perceiving themselves as the target of police attention as opposed to partners in crime prevention.

Evidence on this remains mixed. A study by Hinkle and Weisburd (2008) reported that citizens who lived in residential areas subject to crackdown-style policing activities were more likely to fear crime occurring. On the contrary, a study by Weisburd et al (2010) found that these concerns may be overstated as citizens in their study demonstrated little awareness of increased police attention in their areas and therefore there was no increase in fear.

In deciding whether to implement a problem-oriented approach to a particular issue, you can also apply the **CHEERS** acronym, which can help you understand whether the problem would be suitable for this approach (Clarke and Eck, 2003).

Community – is this issue affecting the community?

Harm – it is causing indirect, or direct, harm?

Expect – does the public expect the police to address this harm?

Events – does it include discrete and clearly defined events?

Recurring – is this a recurring crime issue?

Similar – are similar events occurring in the same location or involving similar individuals?

Don't forget that as each crime is unique, its response is likely to be too. What works in one hot spot location may not work in another; therefore, you should be open to trying out a variety of approaches. You should use the SARA model for each new activity trialled as this will encourage robust evaluation and reflective practice.

If the crime issue does meet the CHEERS criteria, there are additional practical considerations.

1. Identify practical considerations.

    o Are there sufficient officers to conduct the policing activity?

    o How many hot spots will the activity be implemented at and what will this entail?

    o Can officers travel between the different hot spot locations and conduct 15-minute patrols in a time-effective manner?

    o Is any investment required (technology, resources, training etc)?

    o How will you ensure officers remain at the hot spot location for a sufficient length of time?

2. Identify the relevant stakeholders (internally and externally).

    o This will include individuals who are affected by the policing activity, individuals who may be able to support the activity both in terms of resources and in terms of championing the activity, as well as individuals who may be resistant.

REFLECTIVE PRACTICE 2.2

LEVELS 4-6

Reflect upon the skills which you have gathered through your degree in relation to researching problems, working with statistics and analysing data, understanding methodologies, and undertaking research projects. How might these skills help in planning and conducting hot spot policing activities?

Sample answers are provided at the end of this book.

ETHICAL CONSIDERATIONS

COMMUNITY TENSIONS

As discussed, increased police attention in high-crime areas can sometimes have a negative impact on police–community relations. This may arise from several factors such as citizens' frustrations with ongoing crime concerns in their area or a scepticism of the police and their increased attention in that area. While some citizens may perceive increased foot patrols as reassuring, others may perceive it as more intrusive and may consider that they are being unfairly subjected to police surveillance. This could increase tensions with local communities and even alienate citizens.

REFLECTIVE PRACTICE 2.3

LEVELS 5 AND 6

You have been asked to increase foot patrols on an inner-city road in Manchester which has been identified as a burglary hot spot. The road has a high proportion of residents of Pakistani heritage. You had expected your foot patrols to be welcomed but you are met with resistance from citizens on the street. What would you say to the citizens to explain your presence on the street? How would you allay their concerns that they were being disproportionately targeted?

Sample answers are provided at the end of this book.

However, it is possible to mitigate tensions which may arise from increased police activity in hot spot locations. A study by Ariel et al (2016) suggested that increased patrols by PCSOs had a successful crime reduction effect. Where the benefits of hot spot policing can be achieved through 'soft' policing methods, this may be a more effective strategy.

Weisburd et al (2021) found that training officers in procedural justice meant that hot spot policing methods could be successfully implemented and produce crime reduction effects while preserving positive public opinion of the police. The procedural justice model identifies four key elements which can help to strengthen citizen satisfaction during police–citizen encounters.

- **Dignity and respect** – have you treated the citizen with dignity and respect?

- **Voice** – can you allow citizens the opportunity to participate in the encounter? For example, by actively listening to them, by offering them an opportunity to explain or to express their concerns etc.

- **Explanation** – have you explained why you are exercising your powers in that manner? Does your explanation demonstrate neutrality and equality in your decision making?

- **Trustworthy motives** – do you demonstrate care and concern for the citizen in a manner indicative of trustworthy motives?

Procedural justice is one of the strongest predictors of citizens' perceptions of police legitimacy; therefore, if you can demonstrate the above elements in your encounters with citizens, this may mitigate some of the potentially damaging consequences of hot spot policing.

REFLECTIVE PRACTICE 2.4

LEVELS 5 AND 6

You are part of a team adopting hot spot policing methods to address an ongoing concern with disorder and drugs usage occurring around three blocks of flats situated within 50 metres of each other. One of the tactics your team is using is increased police stops. While on patrol in the area, you observed two males exchange a small package although you did not see what this consisted of. Upon spotting you and your colleague, the two males ran away. When you caught up with the males, you decided to conduct a stop and search.

- How could you incorporate the procedural justice model into your stop and search?

- Read the guidance on fair and effective communication from the College of Policing and reflect on how you could incorporate this into your own stop and search practice: www.college.police.uk/app/stop-and-search/fair.

Sample answers are provided at the end of this book.

SUMMARY OF KEY CONCEPTS

This chapter has explored the following key concepts.

- Hot spot policing provides a data-led targeted approach to crime reduction by focusing upon micro-locations.

- The evidence base on hot spot policing suggests it can be a very effective strategy.

- A wide array of policing activities has been trialled at hot spot locations; therefore, although we know that targeting activities to specific locations works, we do not yet understand which activities are the most effective.

- Two main approaches to hot spot policing include increased patrols and problem-oriented policing strategies.

- There is a range of factors which forces should consider prior to adopting a hot spot policing activity, including training needs, resources and ensuring internal and external stakeholders have been considered.

- Increased police attention can, however, have a negative impact on police–community relations; this can be mitigated through 'soft' policing methods and the adoption of a procedurally just approach.

- As hot spot policing is an increasingly relied upon strategy, it is likely that you will encounter this policing method at some point in your career. You should keep yourself up to date with emerging research which develops your understanding of hot spot policing.

CHECK YOUR KNOWLEDGE

1. Can you define hot spot policing?

2. Can you provide five examples of policing activities associated with hot spot policing?

3. What is the suggested duration that police patrols should be conducted for?

4. What does the term 'spatial crime displacement' mean and why is this considered a risk of hot spot policing?

5. What is the procedural justice model and how can you apply it to your interactions with the public?

Sample answers are provided at the end of this book.

FURTHER READING

ARTICLES, BOOKS AND CHAPTERS

Basford, L, Sims, C, Agar, I, Harinam, V and Strang, H (2021) Effects of One-a-Day Foot Patrols on Hot Spots of Serious Violence and Crime Harm: A Randomised Crossover Trial. *Cambridge Journal of Evidence Based Policing*, 5: 119–33.

Braga, A A, Turchan, B S, Papachristos, A V and Hureau, D (2019) Hot Spots Policing and Crime Reduction: An Update of an Ongoing Systematic Review and Meta-Analysis. *Journal of Experimental Criminology*, 15: 289–311.

Sherman, L and Eck, J (2002) Police for Crime Prevention. In Sherman, L, Farrington, D, Welsh, B and Layton MacKenzie, D (eds) *Evidence-Based Crime Prevention*. London: Routledge (pp 295–329).

Weisburd, D and Eck, J E (2004) What Can Police Do to Reduce Crime, Disorder and Fear? *The Annals of the American Academy of Political and Social Science*, 593: 42–65.

WEBSITES

College of Policing (2018) Crime Reduction Toolkit: Hot Spots Policing. [online] Available at: www.college.police.uk/research/crime-reduction-toolkit/hot-spots-policing (accessed 24 February 2023).

College of Policing (2023) Problem-Solving Policing. [online] Available at: www.college.police.uk/guidance/problem-solving-policing (accessed 20 March 2023).

CHAPTER 3
PREDICTIVE POLICING

LEARNING OBJECTIVES

AFTER READING THIS CHAPTER YOU WILL BE ABLE TO:

- define predictive policing;

- explain and apply the predictive policing cycle model to a range of practical policing scenarios;

- explore the strengths and limitations of predictive policing and how this knowledge may support your decision making and operational judgement;

- recognise the ways in which data can be collected and where data can be sourced from;

- utilise a range of open-source crime mapping sites to explore the levels of crime in a particular location;

- consider the ethical implications of predictive policing.

INTRODUCTION

Predictive policing '*is sweeping the nation, promising the holy grail of policing – preventing crime before it happens*' (Ferguson, 2017, p 1109) and is a modern policing method that endeavours to predict where crime may occur and support decision makers with the allocation of resources to deal with it before it has a chance to take hold. Crucially, predictive policing does not replace other policing methods such as hot spot policing but enhances the more traditional practices (National Institute of Justice, 2014) through the application of statistical models supported by large quantities of gathered data.

This chapter explores the concept of predictive policing and begins by offering a practical overview of the topic, before focusing on the use of data by the police to analyse, anticipate and respond to future crime and how it can inform daily practice. The practical application of predictive policing will be discussed, informing you of its use in a range of settings such as the ability to identify potential criminal activity in an at-risk area, alongside more operational and strategic uses such as the allocation and deployment of resources in a period of relative austerity. You are encouraged to consider the wide-reaching impact of predictive policing, with particular focus on forecasting for the future, looking at both the associated merits and limitations of the problem-solving model in practice.

The chapter concludes by encouraging you to consider the ethical implications of predictive policing, how it may impact your decision making and professional judgement and challenging you to think critically around the subject, both as a student and within your future careers.

DEFINING PREDICTIVE POLICING

Within the literature, it is difficult to find a unified definition of predictive policing, though there is some consensus on a few of its core features. The most pertinent of these are the use of numerical techniques to forecast or predict when criminal activities may occur (usually a short timeframe and commonly linked to the near future) and how this may impact or influence the decision making of law-enforcement personnel (usually where to send resources).

Predictive policing, alongside other policing trends such as real-time identification and tracking of individuals and the development and merging of a variety of databases (Jansen, 2018), sits under the umbrella of 'data-driven policing' – which is the use of crime data and other intelligence sources to better inform the policing of a vast array of situations. Kirby and Keay (2021) delve deeper into the benefits of data-driven policing, listing the diagnosis of operational and organisational problems, as well as the ability to provide the appropriate information to partners, as key elements of the practice.

Developing some of the core ideas found within the literature, Meijer and Wessels (2019, p 1033) offer the understanding that:

> *Predictive policing is the collection and analysis of data about previous crimes for identification and statistical prediction of individuals or geospatial areas with an increased probability of criminal activity to help developing policing intervention and prevention strategies and tactics.*

From here you can start to understand that predictive policing is therefore a proactive policing model that utilises a range of data and relevant programmes to determine where crime or criminal activity may occur, which in turn will be used by police staff and decision makers to highlight the most relevant places and areas to send officers to or invest resources in. Thus, predictive policing could be said to be concerned with the use of mathematical, analytical and predictive techniques which are designed to identify potential criminal activity within a policing area (Bryant and Bryant, 2019).

This is particularly important to note in the period from 2010 to 2019, where the number of police officers fell by over 20,000 (Statista, 2022a) and therefore deployable resource was arguably at its lowest level since the early 1980s. Therefore, from a practical and operational point of view it makes sense to be able to send officers more accurately to an area which may be subject to criminal acts or intervene in areas where the potential for crime could be high.

In order to deepen your understanding of the topic it is worth further underpinning two of the core features of predictive policing.

1. **The use of a broad range and variety of data** – as predictive policing focuses on descriptive data analytics (analysing data to find causes, insights and trends), the greater the number of potential sources and data streams that can be used, the bigger the picture that can be built by law enforcement agencies, which could in turn support strategic and tactical planning. Traditional policing methods tended to rely on criminal data, which could potentially offer a biased viewpoint, whereas more up-to-date practices source data from a range of areas, such as gang-related affiliations, social network analysis and hot spot data, offering the police a more informed and well-rounded set of information to act upon.

2. **Connection with pre-emptive policing** – one of the core benefits of predictive policing is to enable police forces to act before criminal activities can take place, allowing them to be more forward focused and not kept on the back foot. The use of detailed data allows the police to better pre-empt criminality and when further supported by a range of interconnected organisations (for example, child protection services, intelligence organisations and other police forces) makes it possible for the police to significantly reduce the ability and chances to commit crime.

As stated by Brayne et al (2015), there are four key stages in the practice of predictive policing, which is simply represented in Figure 3.1.

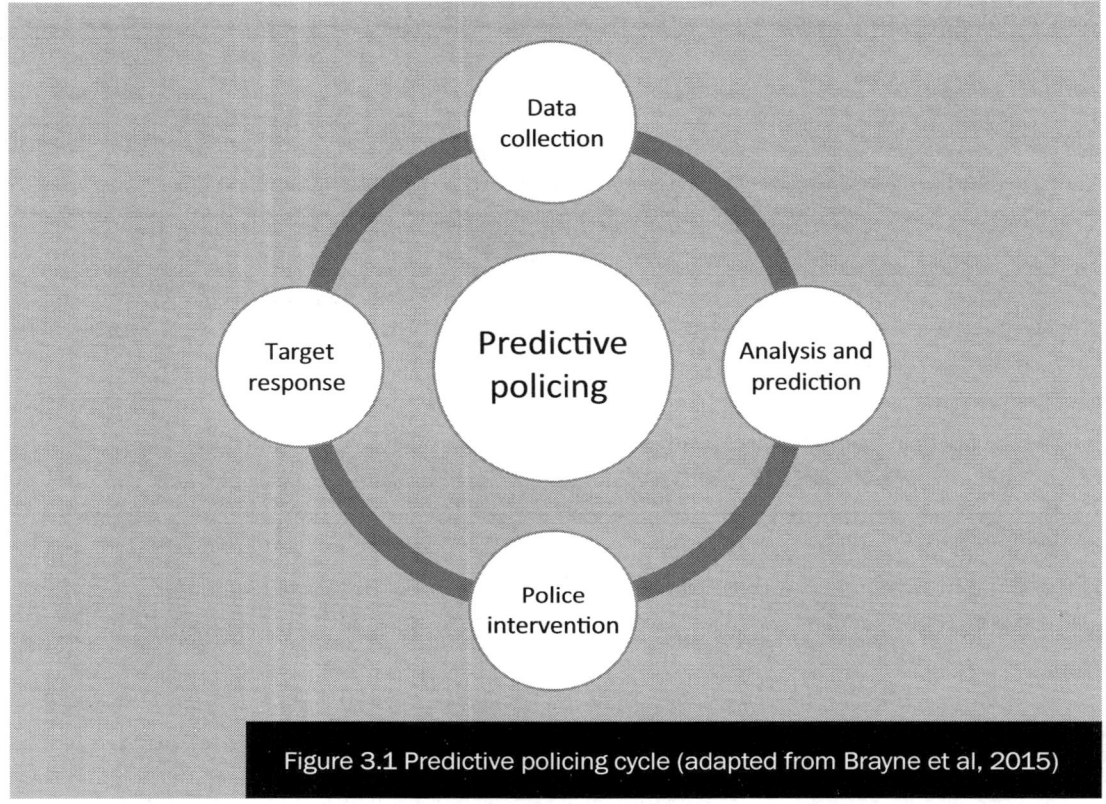

Figure 3.1 Predictive policing cycle (adapted from Brayne et al, 2015)

- **Phase 1** – *data collection* – can range from basic crime data such as where a crime has occurred to more complex and significant information such as the composition of a neighbourhood where crime rates are high, or the locations of high-profile targets such as shopping centres and cash machines.
- **Phase 2** – *analysis and prediction* – here, policing organisations will need to consider the types of crime they want to target and the resources they have at their disposal.
- **Phase 3** – *police intervention* – at this stage, police decision makers will determine who to deploy depending on the nature of the data and intelligence.
- **Phase 4** – *target response* – the final phase is where reflections and learning should take place and needs to account for the impact of the police intervention. For example, if the police tactic was to send additional patrol officers to an area, did this prevent the crime from occurring or simply displace it to another location?

REFLECTIVE PRACTICE 3.1

LEVEL 4

Predictive policing is most associated with location-based predictions, which involves using pre-existing crime data to deploy resources to an area in order to pre-empt the chances of criminal actions taking place. Within your policing career, it is incredibly likely that the practical work you carry out will at some point be driven by predictive policing. Therefore, it is important to understand how to apply the four stages of the predictive policing cycle to a range of pragmatic solutions and resolutions.

SCENARIO 1

A local middle school within your neighbourhood is regularly subjected to vandalism and criminal damage to its outside play equipment. It is on the outskirts of town and is poorly lit, with very low-level fences surrounding it. Recently gathered data has highlighted the school as a location that is likely to be targeted again and you have been tasked to offer a police intervention.

- What steps would you take to limit the impact on the school in the future?

LEVELS 5 AND 6

Another of the core applications of predictive policing is the person-based link, which seeks to predict individuals and groups who are most likely to be involved in crime. Importantly, this includes both offenders and victims and could include individuals with gang affiliations, domestic abuse sufferers or people who are likely to be involved in violent crime. Again, a practical understanding of the predictive policing cycle is beneficial to your role, although the scenario below may require some additional thought due to the nature of the information given.

SCENARIO 2

You have received intelligence from your in-house domestic abuse team that a known victim is once again at high risk and there is the likely need for police intervention.

- How would you manage this scenario and what factors would you consider?

Sample answers are provided at the end of this book.

BENEFITS AND LIMITATIONS OF PREDICTIVE POLICING

Predictive policing, alongside topics such as the disproportionate use of stop and search powers, facial recognition software and the surveillance of the public, is one of the most controversial topics to have faced the police and wider law enforcement communities in recent years and it is likely to remain so as the use of data and artificial intelligence (AI) technology both develops and becomes more commonplace in our daily lives.

As a contentious policing method, there will always be arguments for and against the predictive policing model in practice. For example, the use of personal data is often met with resistance and criticism, as too is the idea that data often doesn't address the underlying cause of a problem. Therefore, it is imperative that the police are mindful of how they communicate and deal with the public during these interactions.

The following section will offer an understanding of both the inherent benefits and potential limitations of predictive policing. It is important for your careers in policing to be mindful of the potential impacts that can be derived from this policing model.

BENEFITS OF PREDICTIVE POLICING

1. **Resources can be deployed more accurately both to a designated place and at a specific time**

    A strength of predictive policing technology is the ability to identify areas that are at an increased level of risk. For example, this could be the area from a train station to a local football ground when matches are being played; the police can utilise both historical crime data and hot spot identification models and determine that a greater police presence will be needed during these times of high activity. While this is a simplistic example, it clarifies the use of predictive data, combined with the resourcing and deployment of officers, in order to tackle a significant rise in the chances of criminality and criminal behaviours being shown during a specific time period.

2. **Identification of individuals that will be involved in an act of crime**

    As explored by Meijer and Wessels (2019), this can relate to both the victim and the offender. Predictive policing techniques can help to identify individuals at risk and take preventative steps to mitigate this. The information obtained from the data has the capacity to look at behavioural patterns and flag people with the capacity to become offenders, as well as those who may have previously been a victim. Perry (2013) also describes how predictive policing data can help to identify groups of people that are at greater risk of a violent outbreak, citing rival gangs and gang shootings as one example. It is then up to frontline officers alongside decision makers to turn this data into operationally viable material that best serves the needs of the public.

3. **Supports organisations by drawing from a wide variety of sources and can provide links between data sets**

    Predictive policing has the capacity to utilise a vast quantity and array of sources which serves to make the police better informed. Information pertaining to hot spot locations, crime trends, sex offenders, gang affiliations, social services and criminal networks (to name but a few) are used in algorithmic calculations and subject to sophisticated analysis, which in turn is fed into strategic and operational decision making.

EVIDENCE-BASED POLICING

A recent article in *The Conversation* (2022) explores success with predictive policing as seen in both the United States and UK and makes recommendations that the South African law enforcement community should employ similar measures to tackle its problem with crime. The article cites how one US police department were able to reduce gun-related incidents by 47 per cent during the New Year's Eve period and details how Greater Manchester Police were able to decrease burglaries, robberies and thefts from motor vehicles by a significant percentage when utilising predictive policing methods.

LIMITATIONS OF PREDICTIVE POLICING

1. **Automated services** – one of the functions of predictive policing is the automation of a range of analytical tasks that may have previously been carried out by a human analyst, and while this may free up resources to be deployed elsewhere, '*automation could bypass and/or deteriorate human expertise*' (Leese, 2021, p 153). Here, the argument is that without a human link, some of the intricacies of the role may become diminished, plus there is the chance for officers to become deskilled and disincentivised.

2. **Most predictive policing models are mainly data driven and not theory driven** – this links to the above point and to the appropriateness of the models used in practice. There is a chance for a skewed image to be presented: algorithms cannot apply the human insight to the data in front of them and therefore may not give a true depiction of an individual or problem.

3. **Can lead to officer/predictive bias** – if data is already biased then it is likely to remain so (Sandhu and Fussey, 2021). For example, stop and search data already shows that the police disproportionately stop and search young black males – when linked to predictive policing data, it could in turn suggest that more young black males should be targeted for certain crime types, thus exacerbating the problem and not finding a resolution.

4. **Offers false impressions** – this could be putting officers on high alert or offering a false sense of security and could cause a disparity in or influence over officer decision making. For example, if the data states that the subject is a violent offender, then the police tactic or approach to dealing with the individual has the potential to come across as heavy-handed.

5. **It predicts the obvious** – it is likely that certain crimes will always happen in certain areas, such as retail theft always being concentrated in high streets and shopping centres; therefore, predictive policing may get less respect from officers on the ground.

COLLECTING INFORMATION AND DATA

Within your future policing careers, you will have the opportunity to gather and collect information and data on a significant scale – the nature of your role means that you will invariably be involved in the process either through traditional policing methods or as part of planned operations. As the accuracy of data (Ferguson and Picknell, 2022) is tantamount to the success of intelligence gathering and information processing, it is a core skill that you should look to develop and is an aspect of policing you should take care and pride in.

The College of Policing (2023b) states that information collected for one policing purpose may well add value to another and, as such, should be treated as a corporate resource. This helps to underpin the value that policing organisations place on their information and how it can later feed into predictive policing processes. Within the police and other law enforcement agencies, information is largely collected in the following three ways.

1. **Routine collection** – this is most closely linked to the 'bread and butter' work of operational police officers and the information is usually relevant to the purpose for which it was collected. An example of this could be recording the details of a person who was arrested for traffic offences.

2. **Tasked information** – here, priority is placed on collecting information for an intended purpose and is often used by the police to help close a gap in knowledge. For example, this could be the need to find out the location of a vulnerable person who has gone missing from a care facility.

3. **Volunteered information** – commonly collected from members of the public, contacts within the local community as well as partnership agencies. The sharing of information with the police from organisations such as social services is a good example here.

See the link within the further reading section for more details on the collection and recording of information.

REFLECTIVE PRACTICE 3.2

LEVEL 5

- Within the boxes in Table 3.1, write down as many examples as you can of the different ways that information can be collected by the police. Consider the different roles and departments within the police, what members of the public may want to tell the police about and what may motivate them to share information, as well as considering other organisations who work alongside the police.

Table 3.1 Types of information collection

Routine collection	Tasked information	Volunteered information

SOURCES OF DATA

To further embed the importance and impact of data collection on the role of the police, it is worth considering other avenues of data collection. As well as the examples you gave for the previous task, there are a range of other sources of data that you may or may not have considered. The following list suggests several sources, though is in no way exhaustive.

Also, it is realistic to believe that as technological platforms develop and grow, new means of gathering data will grow alongside them.

1. **ANPR cameras** – both those used by the police, as well as those used by organisations such as local authorities. According to Police.uk (2023), all the ANPR cameras in the country submit approximately 60 million ANPR read records per day to national ANPR systems. Searches carried out on ANPR systems will help to identify vehicles involved with offences such as drug distribution and terrorism and can significantly speed up police investigations.

2. **CCTV cameras** – it has been estimated by Clarion Security Systems (2022) that there are over 7 million CCTV cameras in operation in the UK, which equates to roughly 1 camera to every 11 people. In more populous locations (bigger towns and cities) it is likely that the average person will be recorded by CCTV cameras up to 70 times per day.

3. **Social media platforms** – as the demand and membership of social media platforms has grown at an alarming rate, figures suggesting that 4.76 billion people worldwide (Statista, 2023) have an online presence (well over 50 per cent of the population) highlight the need for the police to see social media as an information-sharing and data-collection source. The Police Foundation (2014) split how the police can use social media into three distinct ways.

    a) **Providing information** – very commonly seen on social media platforms such as Twitter, the police utilise these sources to share information quickly and easily and at a very low cost. Information shared includes missing person details, crime safety advice and success stories and it reaches a wide audience instantly.

    b) **Engagement** – it is necessary for the police to reach out to their neighbourhoods and communities to build relationships and gain support for the work they do.

    c) **Intelligence and investigation** – social media accounts can support the intelligence and investigation efforts of the police, ranging from supporting on active cases by asking for the public's CCTV or camera footage, deployment decisions in areas of unrest, to exploiting social media platforms and sites known for criminal and anti-social behaviours.

4. **Stop and search records** – a core aspect of frontline policing is the active involvement in stop and search practices, and a total of 526,024 stop and searches were recorded for the year ending 31 March 2022 (Gov.uk, 2022). Stop and search recording is usually split into three areas: 1) stop and search, 2) stop and account and 3) vehicle stops, feeding into various police databases that can go on to inform future predictive policing measures.

5. **Drones** – within several professions, but in particular law enforcement and the military, there has been a significant rise in the use of drones in recent years. With a number of core benefits such as value for money (far cheaper than using a helicopter), ability to access hard-to-reach places and the ability to live-broadcast events such as football matches, it is clear that they have a genuine place within practical policing tools. As stated by West Midlands Police (2022), they are a useable resource that can be used in crime hot spot areas and serious incidents and have the ability to capture vital evidence and data, thus providing further potential to be involved in predictive policing efforts.

OTHER PROACTIVE POLICING MODELS

As both society and technology have developed, so too have the means for tackling crime and criminal activity; when combined with a reduction of officers on the street, this means that police resources have been more stretched than ever. From a practical perspective, it has been necessary to steer away from *reactive policing* – responding to events as and when they happen – with more emphasis placed on *proactive policing* – taking steps to stop crime before it occurs.

While a core aspect of policing will always be to react to events as they unfold, the development and use of proactive models of policing has been at the core of policing organisations across the globe since the 1960s (Weisburd and Majmundar 2018) and developed in response to a number of pertinent factors such as lack of confidence in the police, rising crime rates and questions around the effectiveness of the standard model of policing (explored below). The 1980s and 1990s saw the police develop more innovative ways of tackling crime, improving police–community relations and winning back trust, recognising that a number of criticisms stemmed from being reactionary – hence the move towards proactiveness.

Proactive policing itself is not a model of policing but is used as an umbrella term that relates to any policing strategy that as a core function looks to reduce or prevent crime with a forward-looking approach (avoiding simply being reactive). It considers the following elements.

- Places an emphasis on crime prevention.

- Uses police initiative to mobilise and distribute resources.

- Seeks to target the underlying causes that may be driving up the rates of crime and disorder.

PROBLEM-ORIENTED POLICING

Problem-oriented policing (POP) was developed by Herman Goldstein in 1979, following his critique that as an organisation the police were too focused on the 'means' of policing rather than the 'ends'; he felt that it was necessary to shift from an older style of policing to one more in keeping with the demands of modern society. The basic premise of POP as detailed by Joyce (2011) is the ability to effectively deal with underlying and recurrent police problems, rather than reacting to incidents as and when they occur. Fundamentally, the POP model is geared towards neighbourhood policing and improving community experiences by shifting the onus away from police decision makers and more towards frontline officers who have a better grasp of the problems and, therefore, better ways to come to a resolution.

INTELLIGENCE-LED POLICING

'*Intelligence-led policing did not originate out of thin air as a new conceptual way of conducting the business of policing*' (Ratcliffe, 2018, p 50). It was developed over a period of time, building on learned experience from the past, combined with an organisational paradigm shift (a new or different approach) towards alternative models of policing. Traditionally, the police had followed the 'standard model of policing' – in essence, random police patrols, rapid response and deployment of officers once a crime had been recorded or detected, followed by the use of the legal system for convictions – thus bringing down the level of crime.

Intelligence-led policing was introduced in the UK in the 1990s and was a crime-focused model which '*emphasized the countering of crime through detection, disruption, or dissuasion*' (Bryant and Bryant, 2019, p 27) with its underlying principles stemming from a recognition that crime and criminal acts can be understood via patterns and linkages between crimes. Here, clear similarities can be drawn with predictive policing as both a model that is proactive in its actions and one that derives much of its content from the analysis and application of data that later informs operational decisions.

GEOGRAPHIC INFORMATION SYSTEMS AND CRIME MAPPING

Geographic information systems (GIS) emerged as a discipline in its own right (Chainey and Ratcliffe, 2005) in the 1960s, with its beginnings in land use applications such as automatic mapping services for use in areas such as census planning and utilities management. As the technology developed, so too did its range of practical uses, with clear links being drawn with the fields of criminology, policing and crime prevention and the clear relationship and overlapping of the two practices (GIS and crime mapping) formed. While both crime mapping and GIS are explored in more detail below and they are two separate disciplines, it is fair to state that they feed into one another and from a generalist policing viewpoint are clearly interlinked.

CRIME MAPPING

As detailed by Rowe (2018), criminological research has consistently shown that crime is not randomly distributed, but instead tends to unduly impact certain people or populations and concentrate in specific locations. He further underpins this point by arguing that a vast number of victimisation surveys highlight two key points.

1. It is a minority of offenders that commit a disproportionate amount of crime.

2. It is a minority of people and/or locations that experience relatively high levels of crime.

Crime mapping is best understood as being the geographical representation of differing crime levels, differing crime times or the locations of incidents and is often shown as an image like the one in Figure 3.2.

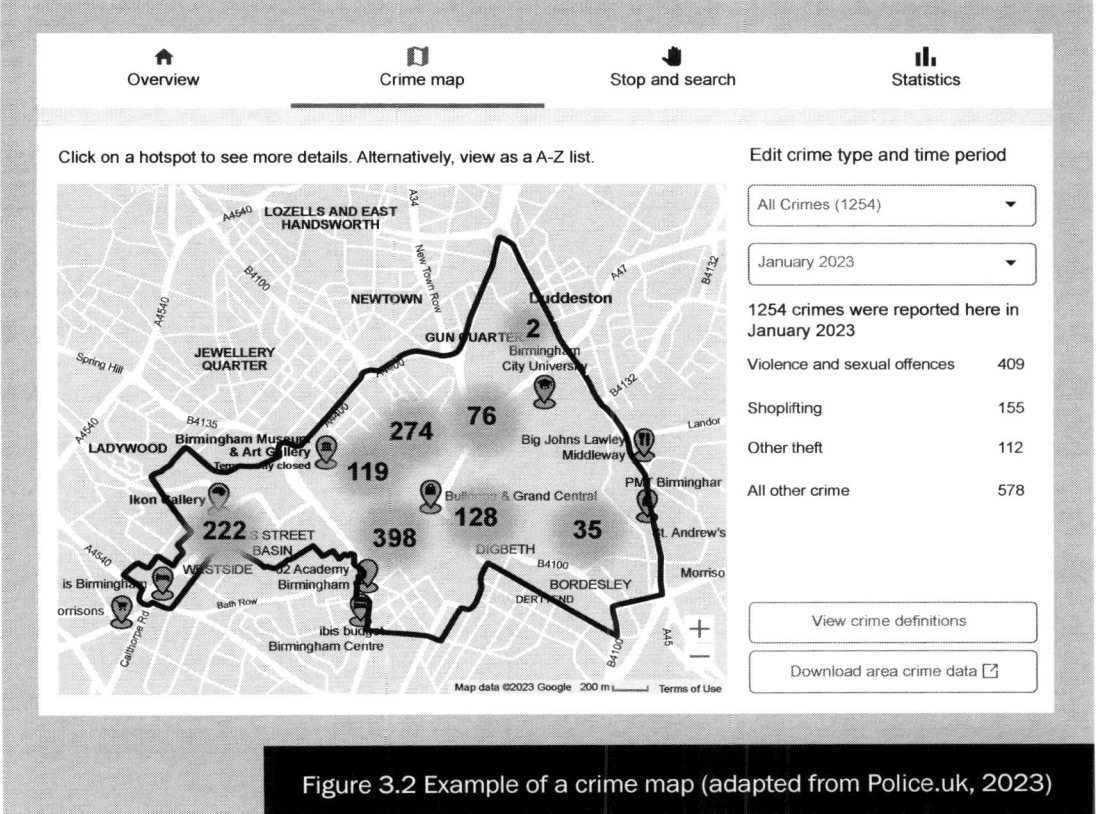

Figure 3.2 Example of a crime map (adapted from Police.uk, 2023)

REFLECTIVE PRACTICE 3.3

LEVEL 4

You may have seen the term 'crime map' being used by your local newspaper or their online news site, where they inform residents about the reported crimes in a particular area or neighbourhood. The sharing of this type of information updates residents with crime-related data, which can be used to safeguard individuals, homes and businesses, as well as supporting police with ongoing investigations.

Before proceeding any further, consider what you know about *crime mapping* and what the term means to you. Then, look to answer the following questions.

- Can you suggest any people, organisations and locations that are at greater risk than others?
- What are the reasons behind your suggestions?
- What purpose does crime mapping serve?

Sample answers are provided at the end of this book.

Since December 2008, all police forces in England and Wales have published their crime statistics via the online crime mapping tool found at www.police.uk – the decision to do so was driven by forces needing to improve the credibility of the crime data that are recorded (Chainey and Thompson, 2012), which in turn should improve the public's trust and confidence in the police. Although crime rates had fallen since the mid-1990s, there was still an underlying feeling of the 'fear of crime', and as such policing organisations needed a way to build confidence in the processes and keep community members informed. Although the new level of transparency shown by the police may have positively impacted some members of society, there are still fundamental issues such as addressing the number of low-level anti-social incidents that may have a greater impact on feelings of safety.

CRITICAL THINKING ACTIVITY 3.1

LEVEL 4

Prior to joining your local police force and therefore to having access to restricted databases such as the Police National Computer (PNC), the Police National Database (PND) and the National DNA Database (NDNAD), take some time to research and explore some of the open-source (available to all) sites that can offer you an insight into crime mapping and statistics. In particular visit www.police.uk and www.ourwatch.org.uk (though there are a range of other options that you may choose to later explore) and input your postcode into the search function. This should provide you with information about the numbers and types of crimes in your local area and will offer you a chance to better understand the type of criminality that occurs in your location.

LEVELS 4, 5 AND 6

Having had the chance to review the crime data in your local area, you are now encouraged to drill down into the information you have found in more detail. For example, can you draw any similarities between violent crime and location? Are the recorded offences concentrated in busier areas such as the local high street or town centre or situated close to pubs and bars?

- Consider some of the other offences that you have found such as theft, anti-social behaviour and shoplifting – what links can you draw from the offence type and location?

- Are there any sections on the crime map that are free from criminality? If so, what could be the reasons behind this?

- Finally, apply this knowledge to Rowe's (2018) theory above – does it appear that certain locations have a higher cluster of reported crimes than others?

Once you have finished looking at the crime mapping data, spend some time working through the other functionalities of the site – there is a range of additional material such as getting to know your local policing team and crime prevention advice that will enhance both your theoretical and practical understanding of policing once you take up a position as a police constable, PCSO or special constable.

POLICING SPOTLIGHT

GRINDR KILLER

Stephen Port, later known as the 'Grindr Killer' is a modern serial killer who took the lives of four men between June 2014 and September 2015 in London. Port predominantly instigated relationships via the Grindr app, luring them to his flat, before poisoning his victims with fatal quantities of the "date rape" drug GHB.

CRITICAL THINKING ACTIVITY 3.2

LEVEL 5

Take some time to use the internet to better familiarise yourself with the Grindr Killer case and visit some of the online maps of the locations where his victims were found.

- Were you surprised by what you saw? What stood out to you?

- To further develop your investigative skills, next carry out your own research into *geographic profiling* (evaluating the locations of serial crimes to best determine probable offender residence) and consider how there are clear links and crossovers with predictive policing. Your research should show how the practice of geographic profiling can be used to support crime analysis efforts and how the mapping of linked crimes and crime sites may support investigators to help pinpoint the most likely location of an offender.

- If Stephen Port hadn't been found as the murderer, do you feel that predictive policing tools could have been used to better support this case? If so, explain how it would have been beneficial and how the police may have used the data.

Sample answers are provided at the end of this book.

GEOGRAPHIC INFORMATION SYSTEMS

As briefly explained earlier in this chapter, GIS has continued to develop over the past 50–60 years with applications ranging from the use of satellite imagery data to support the planning and movements of the military, through to the recognition of patterns in crime to support the organisational, tactical and strategic actions of the police.

The Police Foundation (2006) produced a report that explored the functions of 160 different GIS/crime mapping software products that the police could potentially use in their efforts against crime. They split the products into a number of sub-headings (with a brief description alongside each), based upon the core practical application of the software.

- **Data acquisition/data management** – assists with the purchase/possession of data as well.

- **Geocoding** – products support their users by providing co-ordinates to police data. For example, turning a suspect address into a point on a map.

- **Crime mapping/crime analysis** – allows crime data such as hot spots to be placed onto a map and allows users to visualise and analyse crime patterns.

- **Internet mapping** – tools that support users to view and manipulate data and maps via the internet.

- **Routing software** – allows for detailed directions and efficient trip planning – a common example of this would be delivery drivers working for major supermarkets and online shopping services.

- **Emergency management** – software primarily used for the support of emergency response in both simulation and real-time disasters and major incidents.

ETHICAL CONSIDERATIONS

Wood (2020, p 18) states that '*Ethical policing is competent policing*' and it is this idea that should inspire the next generation of officers. He continues by exploring how police staff should be motivated to act with a 'moral purpose' and to therefore make ethical judgements; it is not simply enough to engage with professional standards of policing. Instead, the argument is that a good deal of reflexive practice is necessary for the development of ethical policing, and it is this concept that should be encouraged for both serving officers and for the new cohorts moving into policing.

It is important to realise that there are a range of limitations associated with predictive policing and if you can help to mitigate and limit some of these occurrences then it will benefit both the individual(s) you are dealing with and the organisation you belong to. Some of the core ethical implications that you could face in your policing role linked to predictive policing are elements such as the appropriate use of data and the consequences that may arise from it. For example, if personal data highlights an individual as someone with the propensity to commit crime and, indeed, they do develop a criminal record, it is likely that they will remain on a variety of databases and categorised as a 'criminal'. In this instance, it is quite possible that the individual concerned may have simply made a few bad choices (often seen in older children) and, rather than being on a database and watch list, needs support, guidance and someone who understands what they may be going through.

REFLECTIVE PRACTICE 3.4

LEVELS 5 AND 6

As part of an assessment for your policing degree, you have been asked to produce a factsheet aimed at your peer group that informs the reader of the core ethical considerations associated with predictive policing. Your factsheet is designed to underpin your subject knowledge, as well as promote critical thinking around the potential impacts of predictive policing, and how this may guide professional judgement and decision making in the future. Take some time to consider the following.

- What elements would you include in your factsheet?

- Why are they important to you?

- How will you get your message across to your peers?

Sample answers are provided at the end of this book.

It is important to note that some scholars (Alikhademi et al, 2021) recognise a need to address some of the limitations of predictive policing, focusing less upon predicting crime or assessing individuals and instead seeking ways to remove the motivations for crime. For example, when individuals are highlighted as having a greater propensity to commit violent acts, a reformed model should focus on public health and initiatives to identify these people and how to support their needs.

CONCLUSION

The purpose of this chapter was to provide an overview of predictive policing – what it is and how it supports the work of the police and law enforcement community in practice – and should offer you the confidence to know how it may impact your roles in the future. Moreover, the chapter was designed to inform you of the capability of the problem-solving model and *'to understand predictive policing so that those using it, or considering it, are aware of its limitations as well as its potential'* (Moses and Chan, 2018, p 13).

It is important to recognise that predictive policing is clearly a tool of the future, but one that needs to be carefully considered. Although it can be argued that the positives largely outweigh the negatives and that it is a viable means to reduce crime and safeguard citizens, the police must be mindful of the potential implications of the data they use. They should be conscious of the underlying reasons why crime may occur and how to support both offenders and victims.

SUMMARY OF KEY CONCEPTS

This chapter has explored the following key concepts.

- Predictive policing is a proactive method of policing that utilises a range of crime-related data from a variety of sources to forecast incidents where crime may occur and where people may be at risk.

- Predictive policing data aids the decision-making process and is most commonly used as a tool that supports managers with the allocation of their operational staff.

- The impact of predictive policing has both positive and negative connotations and it is necessary for all officers to understand what these may be.

- The police gather data by a variety of methods and from a wide range of sources.

- Crime mapping and GIS tools offer a number of opportunities for the police to exploit data, which in turn can support the planning and deployment of officers to a range of scenarios.

- Future officers need to be aware of the potential impact and ethical considerations of predictive policing in practice.

CHECK YOUR KNOWLEDGE

1. What are the two core features of predictive policing?

2. Explain the four stages of the predictive policing cycle and apply them to a chosen scenario.

3. List two benefits and two limitations of predictive policing.

4. According to the College of Policing, what are the three main ways data is collected?

5. Using a simple map, explain the process of crime mapping and how it can benefit the police.

6. Give an example of an ethical limitation of predictive policing and how you would go about mitigating the impact.

Sample answers are provided at the end of this book.

FURTHER READING

ARTICLES, BOOKS AND CHAPTERS

Rossmo, K D (2000) *Geographic Profiling*. Abingdon: Routledge.
This is Rossmo's core text on geographic profiling – in particular, see page 185 onwards.

WEBSITES

College of Policing (2023) Collection and Recording. [online] Available at: www.college.police.uk/app/information-management/management-police-information/collection-and-recording (accessed 23 February 2023).
Comprehensive information exploring the management of police information, and how information is collected, utilised and protected.

Neighbourhood Watch (2023) Crime Map. [online] Available at: www.ourwatch.org.uk/crime-prevention/crime-prevention/crime-map (accessed 24 February 2023).
A useful open-source tool that allows you to gain a greater understanding of the number and types of crime in your neighbourhood.

Police.uk (2023) Welcome to Police.uk. [online] Available at: www.police.uk (accessed 24 February 2023).
The national website for policing in England, Wales and Northern Ireland, which provides crime statistics data, as well as information pertaining to crime prevention and support services.

CHAPTER 4
RATIONAL CHOICE THEORY

LEARNING OBJECTIVES

AFTER READING THIS CHAPTER YOU WILL BE ABLE TO:

- understand the definition of Rational Choice Theory;
- understand the philosophical underpinnings of Rational Choice Theory;
- critically apply Rational Choice Theory to policing practice;
- understand and be able to apply theories which comprise Rational Choice Theory;
- critically reflect upon your own views on the relevance of Rational Choice Theory.

INTRODUCING RATIONAL CHOICE THEORY

There are numerous conceptions of Rational Choice Theory (RCT); however, the core of the concept is that individuals make a decision as to whether to offend or not based on the likely outcome (Thomas et al, 2020). This means that individuals are enticed to offend by potential rewards and may be dissuaded by fear of consequences (Becker, 1968; Nagin, 1998). RCT rests on the idea that people will act in their own best interests and are able to make choices which further these; according to this idea, each decision you make involves a risk/reward calculation (Gul, 2009).

The idea that people can be stopped from offending if the risks outweigh any potential benefit has consequences for the way that the police approach criminality. However, this concept is based on several assumptions which are not universally accepted. These assumptions and their origins are discussed below before the application of RCT and critiques of it are considered.

PHILOSOPHICAL ROOTS

The philosophical beginnings of RCT in criminology date back to the 1700s and the work of Beccaria and Bentham (Smith, 2017). These ideas rested upon the classical criminologist concept that human beings are rational actors who have free will, in other words, that people use logic and can make rational decisions (Burke, 2019). Bentham argued that humans behave in accordance with utilitarian principles: you act to maximise your pleasure and minimise your pain (Bentham, 1983). Beccaria asserted that you could therefore control crime by ensuring that citizens understand that if they commit crime, they will be punished and what those punishments might be (Beccaria, 1995).

Deterrence is a key component of how you understand these ideas. It suggests that if you want something but the punishment for doing it is too severe, you will not attempt it, you will be deterred; this is individual deterrence (Burke, 2019). If your friend has committed the offence and been punished, seeing this will make you want to avoid their fate; this is general deterrence (Burke, 2019). Utilitarianism also provides a moral justification for punishment which goes beyond retribution or revenge: because you should aim for the greatest pleasure and least pain for the greatest number of people, you can justify punishing criminals if this may deter them and reassure the law-abiding majority (Ewing, 1927). A crime-free society would bring us all more pleasure than the collective pain inflicted by punishing all criminals.

The above is a basic introduction to the roots and underpinning ideas of RCT; however, more modern criminologists have tried to apply this more directly to solving society's problems, suggesting specific actions for politicians, the criminal justice system and the police.

RELATED CRIMINOLOGICAL THEORY

The principles of RCT have been adopted to develop modern criminological theories. *Routine Activity Theory (RAT)* and *Situational Action Theory (SAT)* both rely upon the idea that humans are rational and able to conduct a cost–benefit analysis (or weigh the pros and cons) before taking action (Steele, 2015). These modern theories, such as that proposed by Cornish and Clarke (1987), rely upon a more nuanced view of rationality: humans do not have the capacity and time to meticulously calculate before each decision; they also lack full information but can operate under 'bounded rationality'.

REFLECTIVE PRACTICE 4.1

LEVEL 4

For your initial task, think of a few examples when you have made a decision under pressure – these can be examples from your personal, professional and academic life and you are to draw from your own experiences. Do you think you conducted a cost–benefit analysis or did you act with 'bounded rationality' (where you had a limited ability to reason, with factors preventing logical decision making)? What influenced the decisions you made? Once you have considered your own experiences, try and visit the task from a policing perspective. Does this alter the process at all?

Sample answers are provided at the end of this book.

RAT, from Cohen and Felson (1979), holds that crime occurs when three specific factors unite:

1. a motivated offender;

2. a suitable target (or victim);

3. the absence of a capable guardian.

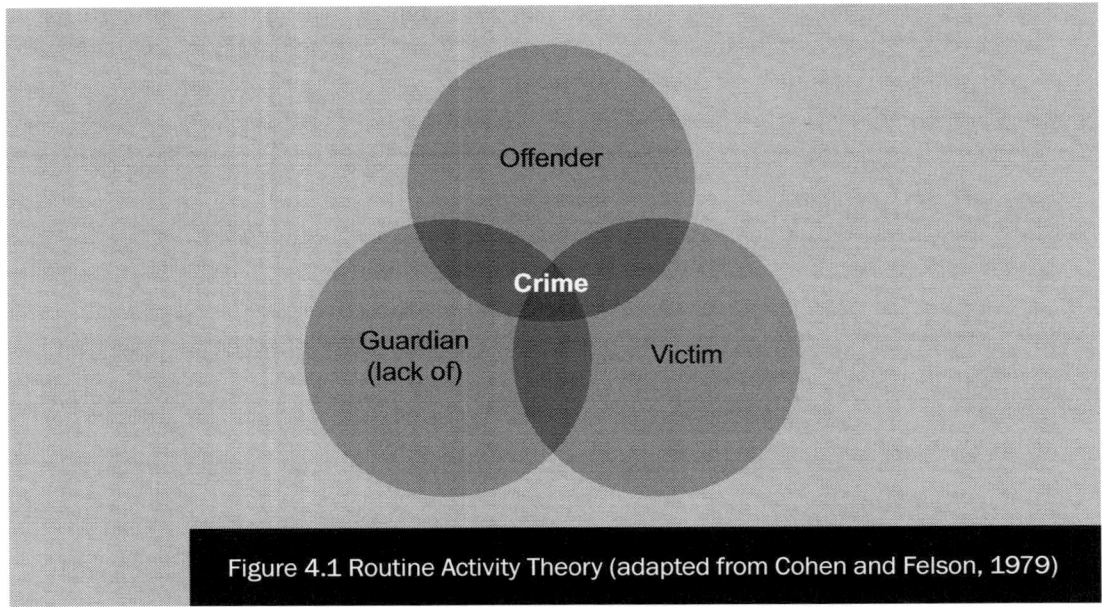

Figure 4.1 Routine Activity Theory (adapted from Cohen and Felson, 1979)

This theory considers the behaviour of both offender and victim; if you remove either of these, a crime will not take place (Cohen and Felson, 1979).

POLICING SPOTLIGHT

Mike is desperate after running up a debt to a loan shark and cannot pay the weekly installments demanded (1). He gets the train to work at 6am with a stranger (Nisha) who is carrying a lot of cash which can be seen in her bag; she is also going to her workplace (2). After they reach their station, they both walk through a dark underpass and rarely see anyone else (3). Mike can snatch Nisha's bag.

Why? Because Mike is present, with motivation to steal (1), Nisha is suitable (vulnerable) with the item he wants (2), and no one (no capable guardian) is there to prevent this (3).

Consider the following changes that could prevent this scenario from happening.

- If Mike is lent money or his loan shark and his gang are imprisoned then Mike is no longer a motivated offender; if Mike is late for work, on holiday or off sick, he is no longer present as a motivated offender. Element (1) is removed.

- If Nisha is off sick from work or on holiday or if she drives to work instead, the suitable victim is absent; if she stops carrying or displaying cash, she is no longer a suitable victim. Element (2) is removed.

- If there are more people walking through the underpass or if someone is with Nisha or there is better lighting or (better still) a police/security presence, a capable guardian is present. Element (3) is removed.

When Mike is absent, or no longer needs the money or the money is not available, he does not offend. If someone demonstrates a strong negative consequence for the crime, he does not offend. He only steals if the benefit outweighs the risk.

Hopefully you see how easily the police can constitute an effective Element (3) but you may also give advice to remove Element (2) and be involved in early intervention to remove Element (1). Application of these theories to policing will be discussed in greater detail later in the chapter.

SITUATIONAL ACTION THEORY

SAT is also part of RCT criminology; according to Wikström and Treiber (2018), it assumes the following.

- People are basically guided by rules; you express your wants and respond to stress in this context.

- Social order is based on norms which are mutually agreed social rules which guide routines and social behaviour.

- People generate their own actions; they make choices and carry these out.

- Actions differ depending on the situation; the context influences perception of the available options, the process of choosing from these and how you perform them. You interact with your environment to make a decision.

- Crimes are moral actions which contravene the law, which guides us as to right or wrong in a particular context.

SAT uses three explanatory mechanisms: *situational, selection* and *emergence* mechanisms, as well as a *PEA hypothesis* and consideration of factors which contribute to changes in offending (Wikström, 2017, pp 513–16; Wikström, 2018).

1. **Situational mechanism** (**perception-choice process**) explains why this offending happens.

2. **Selection mechanism** (processes of **social and self-selection**) explains why the situations in which offending may occur come to be.

3. **Emergence mechanism** (person and social emergence) explains why people (through psychosocial processes) and places (through socio-ecological processes) change, in relation to the cause of crime.

4. People basically commit acts of crime because they believe them to be justifiable in a particular context and there is not a suitable **deterrent** or because they neglect their own morals (for example, lose their temper) in circumstances where they experience external pressure.

KEY STEPS IN THE ACTION PROCESS

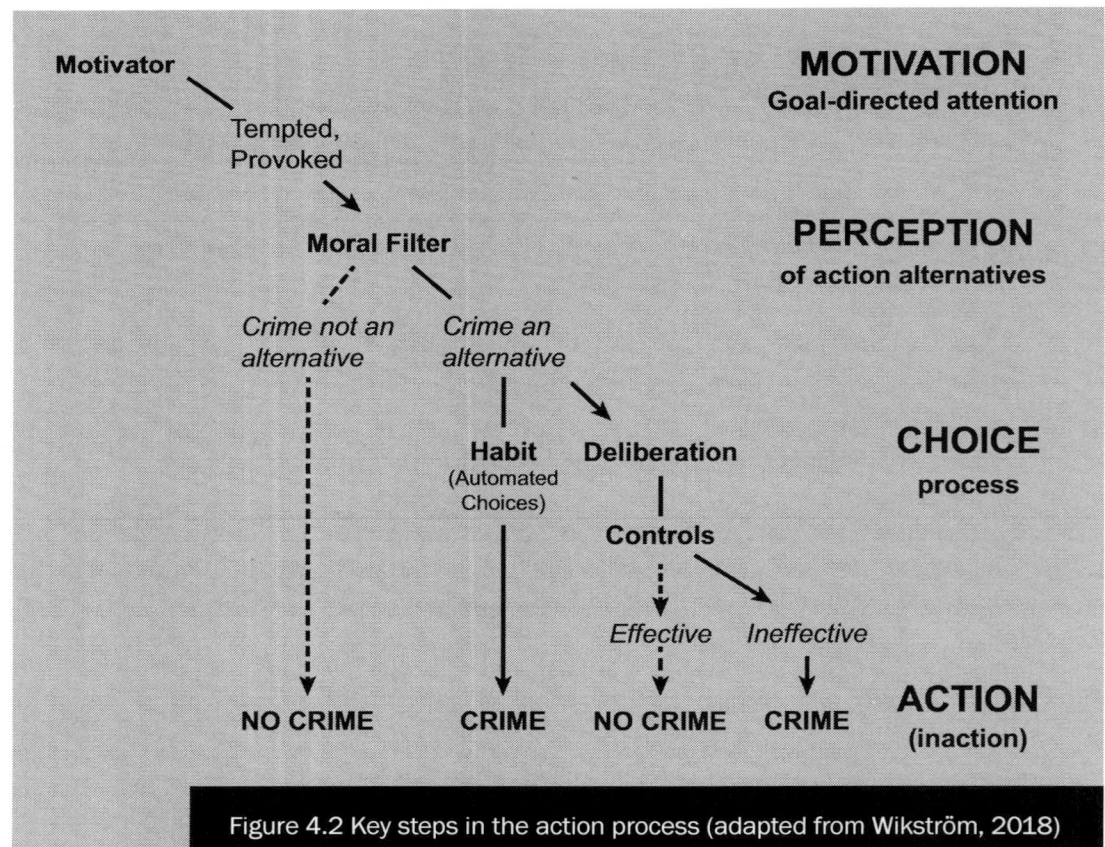

Figure 4.2 Key steps in the action process (adapted from Wikström, 2018)

The **PEA hypothesis** (**P** × **E** → **A**) asserts that an offence (**A**) is an outcome of the perception-choice process (→), which begins and is guided by interaction (×) between people's crime propensities (likelihood of committing it) (**P**) and the immediate environment's criminogenic inducements (persuasive factors) (**E**) in response to a unique motivation. Crimes are therefore an outcome of unique combinations of individuals (propensities) in specific places (inducements).

- The action process is initiated when a **motivator** (or temptation) provides goal-directed attention. Motivation is situational and necessary but not enough alone to create action.

- What available options the person sees is dependent upon **moral filtering** (which occurs when personal morals are applied to the motivator). The moral filter is contextual (or situational).

- If a person doesn't see crime as a viable choice, no crime occurs, even though the ability to make that decision remains.

- A **choice** is a combination of an intention to act in this situation or context. Whether crime is seen as a viable choice in response to a motivator is dependent upon the choice process. Circumstances dictate where this choice is just habit or a considered, rational choice.

- To act according to **habit** is to react in accordance with stimulus-response and environmental cues. The person only perceives one viable action alternative (although they may know they technically have a choice). Habitual choices are created by relying on past experience. Habits are created by frequent exposure to similar situations and mostly occur in familiar circumstances with similar rules or in high stress/emotional situations.

- When a person perceives multiple viable choices, they become **rationally deliberative**. Deliberations focus on the future and assessment of the best outcome (crime only occurs if it seems like the best chance of the best outcome). SAT argues the best option is the most realistic and morally acceptable method to achieve goals (not necessarily the one that is seen to maximise personal advantage or gain). When people deliberate, they use 'free will' within the constraints of the choices available. The level of deliberation varies according to the perceived importance of the choice. Rational deliberation is most usual when people are in unfamiliar circumstances and/or there is conflicting rule guidance.

- **Controls** are influences which oppose something to support an alternative; this differs depending on the context. This only matters when deliberation, based on conflicting rules, occurs.

- **Controls** can be internal (self-control) or external (deterrence) in origin. The exercise of self-control only occurs if the person may otherwise have offended in that situation.

CRITICAL THINKING ACTIVITY 4.1

LEVEL 6

The PEA hypothesis above provides you with an understanding of why crime events happen and considers a range of impacting factors such as the presence of a motivator, moral filtering and choices, plus a range of controls that may impact the decision to commit crime or not. Take the time to identify the answers to the following questions.

- What controls are you all subject to in society?

- What specific controls would stop a police officer from mistreating a suspect?

- How do the police play a role in the 'rational deliberation' of citizens?

Sample answers are provided at the end of this book.

CHANGES WHICH PREVENT OFFENDING IN SAT

- Changes in offending are caused by changes in people's crime propensities and their exposure to environments which promote committing crime.

PERSONAL CHANGES (ALTERING CRIME PROPENSITIES)

- Changes in biology which impact self-control and/or decision making.

- Changes driven by moral instruction and cognitive teaching (values taught and ideas imparted) because people's crime propensities come from morals within a legal context.

- Changes in these will occur due to changes in the environment as you react to them.

RATIONAL CHOICE THEORY

ACTIVITY FIELD CHANGES (INFLUENCING CRIMINOGENIC EXPOSURE)

- Changes in exposure to situations are driven by changes in chosen activity and social selection (based on social norms and resources). A person's activity field is the setting they usually participate in.

- Changes in agency (powers to make changes) are driven by internal and external changes, while people's development of and changes in activity preferences are driven by their experiences of such activities.

- External changes (eg political, economic, technical or cultural) may impact the nature and frequency of available settings (in a jurisdiction) or rules regarding the availability of resources, relevant to a particular person making decisions in a certain setting.

POLICING SPOTLIGHT

RETURNING TO THE EARLIER EXAMPLE – APPLYING THE PEA HYPOTHESIS

- Mike's perceived **motivator** is wanting Nisha's money.

- Based on his **moral filtering** and in this context, committing this crime is the best option. Mike may fear he and his family will be targeted if he does not secure the money; it is better that he steals than his wife or sister are attacked. He may not perceive another viable choice.

- His **choice** to offend is based upon his limited options, the ease with which the crime could be committed and the lack of need for additional violence. It could also be because he has experienced different moral instruction and cognitive teaching, such as seeing criminality role modelled as propensity for crime can be impacted by morals as well as desperation.

- This high-stress situation could make Mike act upon **habit** and recall previous instances of being targeted by his loan shark and thus he is seeking to avoid the same outcome.

- However, Mike may acknowledge multiple viable choices and be **rationally deliberative**. He may use his free will to choose to steal rather than report the

→

loan shark to the police (which he views as unlikely to work in the immediate term) or risk being assaulted.

- He may experience discomfort due to competing **controls**; he may see 'grassing' as wrong because he knows he took the money of his own 'free will' but also not wish to break the law. His guiding principles are in conflict, meaning he must go against one of them to achieve the primary outcome of keeping himself and his family safe.

- Mike's controls may come from both his internal guilt and deterrence; he may fear being arrested or recall what happened to a friend when he disappointed the loan shark.

CRITICAL THINKING ACTIVITY 4.2

LEVEL 4

- Take a minute to write down two to four differences in circumstances that might prevent the offence mentioned in the policing spotlight above, and then check your ideas against the bullet points below.

    o Mike may visit a friend or family member who could say something that reminds him he has been taught (and always agreed) that stealing is wrong; someone he loves may be mugged, prompting him to refocus on possible unintended impacts.

    o He might find himself not seeing Nisha for a few days after missing that train and thus be unable to carry out the crime immediately and feel less focused on that course of action in the longer term.

    o He could increase his agency, either through finding another avenue to secure the money or gaining the ability to move out of the area, thus moving away from danger from the loan shark.

    o The environment may change: there may be a greater presence from the Transport Police owing to unconnected circumstances; lighting in the underpass may improve; new posters reminding people of CCTV/very visible cameras may be introduced, thus increasing the deterrent element; the loan shark may move away or be imprisoned.

RATIONAL CHOICE THEORY   75

> - Nisha may stop travelling alone, make it clear she is due to meet someone or cease to appear to carry large sums of money.
>
> - Identify two to four potential opportunities for the police to prevent crime, according to RCT. You will now explore these in greater detail.
>
> *Sample answers are provided at the end of this book.*

APPLICATION TO CRIME PREVENTION

The ideas put forward by RCT have had a profound impact on the current criminal justice system (Steele, 2015). To explore this, it is important to examine first the impact upon legislation and policy which guides the police service and then the implications for operational policing.

HISTORICAL INFLUENCE ON POLICY: ASBOs AND THE 'SHORT, SHARP SHOCK'

In the 1980s, moral panics (see below) around youth offending led to the development of Thatcher's 'short, sharp shock' policy, designed to frighten criminality out of young offenders. The idea was that the experience of early imprisonment with a harsh regime (including strict rules and an emphasis on physical and mental fitness and discipline) would be so unpleasant that it would frighten criminality out of them. In reality, this deterrence-based policy was described by those directly impacted as brutalising and was statistically ineffective (Dearden, 2018). Nevertheless, it served the purpose of reassuring the public that the criminal justice system made sure that young people were disincentivised from committing crime.

Later, under Tony Blair, anti-social behaviour orders (ASBOs) were introduced as a response to a moral panic about anti-social behaviour. They were widely criticised as a political response to a social and criminological problem, described as a 'badge of honour' for some young people that also deepened class divisions as they were associated with terms like 'chav', which were used as slurs against the working class (Squires, 2008). Although ASBOs succeeded in sending the message that the state (including the police) cared about the right for law-abiding citizens to be free from disruption and intimidation (justice being seen to be done), they ultimately failed to provide a rationale for not committing low-level offences; although an ASBO was a social penalty for some, others could gain social benefit from receiving one. They were also seen as a criminalisation of behaviour which would have been previously thought of as annoying. This presents us with an interesting contradiction: RCT is based on people making sensible choices, but policy often involves intruding in people's lives (Squires, 2008).

MORAL PANIC

A moral panic is when society becomes overly concerned that something is a threat to the values, welfare or safety of the community (Cohen, 2011). Moral panics are usually influenced by the media and sometimes politicians. It may be that there is something genuinely worrying happening, but the focus on, and fear associated with, the particular person, group or cultural phenomena, is disproportionate.

EXAMPLES OF LEGISLATION INFLUENCED BY RATIONAL CHOICE THEORY

The deterrence-focused principles of RCT necessitate potential criminals clearly understanding the potential consequences for their actions. This was one motivation for the introduction of minimum sentences for very serious offences, with the idea that this would send a clear message that the state would not tolerate such behaviour and that the punishment would cause more pain than the pleasure of the crime would provide. These laws have had positive and negative impacts (Fitz-Gibbon, 2016). Despite popularity and the ability to send a message that the state will protect citizens, these policies make it more difficult to sufficiently take into account unusual and mitigating circumstances. As you shall see, this is a key critique of RCT and the policy and practice it influences.

THE INFLUENCE OF RATIONAL CHOICE THEORY ON POLICING PRACTICE

The police have been used as a deterrent. The very presence of officers is seen as preventing crime, as criminals can rationally assume they may be caught and thus punished, altering the circumstances of would-be offenders (SAT) and providing a 'suitable guardian' (RAT). However, this focus also allowed for numbers of officers to be cut. An emphasis on deterrence as opposed to reassuring victims or proactive case work may give the impression that technology (such as CCTV) can allow for reduced numbers while still reducing crime, as long as officers are deployed strategically (Davenport, 2010).

CRITIQUES OF RATIONAL CHOICE THEORY: THEORY AND PRACTICE

THEORETICAL UNDERPINNINGS OF CRITIQUES

There are numerous theoretical critiques of RCT (Hayward, 2007). One key argument is that deterrence, a lynchpin of theories such as RAT and SAT, does not work; it is difficult to statistically prove its impact as it is hard to isolate factors which should deter offences, and jurisdictions with harsher penalties (including capital punishment) do not appear to benefit from lower crime rates (Paternoster, 2010). This suggests that despite the logic of RCT and the appealing 'common-sense' message, benefits and potential costs of crime are not the only factors in offending.

The underlying principles of RCT suggest that in a state when crime is punished with imprisonment, a person would only commit offences where the pleasure gained is incredibly high and/or where they assume it is unlikely they will be caught. This does not appear to be the case. Individuals often appear to be driven by emotion or seeking specific sensations, knowing that these might be fleeting; in many offences there appears to be a clear lack of logical analysis. Moreover, there are individual differences between people. As Wilson and Herrnstein (1985) note, personality differences, including such factors as impulse control, impact how people operate day to day, including whether they commit offences. In short, humans are not all equally rational actors and not only does RCT neglect the role of emotion for all of us, but it also ignores our individuality, including the struggles of vulnerable people.

IGNORING INDIVIDUALITY: LACK OF CONSIDERATION FOR SPECIFIC CIRCUMSTANCES?

RCT assumes rationality and therefore does not aid our understanding of those who find their ability to make logical decisions limited by mental health issues. It is increasingly understood that there is not a binary divide between complete psychological well-being and criminal insanity but rather that mental illness is complex and can impact people in a variety of ways. Many people who would be fit to stand trial may still find their judgement is impacted by a diagnosable condition, such as anxiety or even more serious illnesses such as bipolar disorder. A person's free will can be limited by mental disorders, which can impact their capacity to reason in the same way as the 'average' person (Meynen, 2010).

There may also be other factors which impact an adult's ability to make their own decisions, even if they have no underlying mental health condition. Society has only recently begun to understand the impacts of coercive control. This involves a person abusing another through controlling them, making them feel dependent upon the abuser and therefore unable to make their own decisions (Barlow and Walklate, 2022). In such a situation, are you really able to offer that person a logical choice regarding offending? For example, a person is aware that they will receive a custodial sentence for handling stolen goods and refusing to do so may in fact result in emotional cruelty from their partner and no loss of access to their children (which would occur in prison): logic urges an individual to opt for disappointing the partner over the prison sentence. However, gaslighting and abuse can prevent that person from thinking logically and they may not be in a position to make that rational choice. The emotional impact of the response from the partner in this context, even if there is not a history of physical abuse, may be hard to quantify and thus to include in an accurate cost–benefit analysis.

Other factors may also impact a person's ability to think logically, including addictions such as substance abuse, gambling, pornography or shopping, which may lead to desperation that can inhibit the ability to make rational decisions (Russell, 2021). These issues impact the people that officers come into contact with during day-to-day policing.

CRITICAL THINKING ACTIVITY 4.3

LEVEL 5

If you accept the criticisms outlined above, you can see that the implications for policing are wide-ranging. A number of individuals may lack agency (ability to make their own decisions) for the reasons already given. They may also be unable to make their own decisions due to many reasons, including abuse, trafficking, age, exploitation, immigration status (lack of knowledge of legal rights and language barrier) and many others. This has ramifications for their ability to make the logical decision to comply with the police as well as for how the police deploy resources in terms of controlling crime; officers are required to play a role in safeguarding as well as acting as a deterrent, along with doing the real-life work of solving offences already committed. Officers assuming rational capacity where there is none can have serious consequences.

- Consider scenarios in which you may encounter a suspect who lacks agency. Outline and explain these scenarios.

Sample answers are provided at the end of this book.

POLICING SPOTLIGHT

One infamous example is the case of Derek Bentley (Parris, 1991). Bentley (19) was involved in an armed robbery of an abandoned warehouse when his accomplice Christopher Craig (16) shot police officer Sidney Miles and killed him. Bentley was hanged, owing to claims he had incited Craig to shoot and thus influenced him to commit the crime. This conviction was overturned in 1998 owing to misdirection of the jury by the trial judge.

There are many controversies surrounding this case, and facts were disputed among surviving witnesses and suspects, but Bentley was deemed by police witnesses to have made the decision to influence a child to commit a murder, in order to seek revenge or evade capture. This does not hold up to scrutiny. Numerous officers surrounded the pair, and despite being armed with a knife, Bentley showed no aggression when he was restrained by an officer. Most importantly, Derek Bentley lacked an adult's capacity to engage in logical reasoning: He had severe learning difficulties and a mental age of 11. Officers involved were accused of falsifying or coercing a confession and either falsely claiming that Bentley shouted, '*Let him have it, Chris!*' or misconstruing the meaning of this (claiming a plea for surrender was an incitement to kill). Among the numerous ethical issues (which are not the focus of this chapter) was the lack of consideration of his vulnerabilities. This case highlights the potential problems with assuming human adults are competent to make rational decisions: the police approached the case as though an adult aged 19 was manipulating a teenager but the reality was that his ability to rationalise ceased developing at the age of 11. Assumptions regarding ability to rationalise can lead the police to act upon false beliefs when the truth could drastically change the perception of a suspect.

CRITICAL THINKING ACTIVITY 4.4

LEVELS 4, 5 AND 6

A more recent case is that of Sally Challen, who was jailed for murder in 2011 after killing her husband, Richard, with a hammer (Bettinson, 2019). The Court of Appeal overturned this conviction in 2019; Sally admitted her offence was manslaughter but owing to her time already served in prison, the Crown Prosecution Service declined to take the case for retrial.

Sally met her husband Richard when she was just 15 and he was 22. She was married to him for 31 years but left owing to his controlling, humiliating behaviour and infidelity. However, she soon pleaded for reconciliation, and they got back together after she agreed to his terms; she killed him after becoming certain he was still seeing other women. Sally was able to provide the police with details in a somewhat detached manner and to them the case appeared to be violent revenge motivated by jealousy. In court, she was presented as controlling and vengeful and was sentenced to a minimum of 22 years. Subsequently, our understanding of coercive control has drastically changed, as did the law in 2015.

Following this change, Sally launched an appeal and came forward with her story, which witnesses corroborated. She described humiliation at her husband openly flaunting his attraction to other women, verbal abuse, financial control and occasional physical attacks including rape (to which there were no witnesses) (Mangan, 2019). This culminated in him agreeing to reconcile only if she signed a contract, which included an agreement to forfeit money she was entitled to in their divorce (which he wished to proceed with despite the alleged reconciliation). Upon realising that Richard asking her to sign a humiliating agreement to such terms was another method of control or humiliation and not a sincere attempt to reconcile, Sally claimed she snapped, and the appeal was able to successfully argue that owing to the years of coercive control, she lacked the capacity to reason and was thus not fully culpable.

You may wonder, as rational individuals, that if Richard was controlling, why did he let Sally go and why she did she wish to return? Coercive control involves creating a dynamic of dependence, where a victim loses the capacity to make their own decisions. Sally had not lived as an independent adult; meeting Richard as a child, he made her decisions until she reached middle age. This dynamic meant she lacked the skillset adults require to function alone and could not operate independently. Despite a lack of mental health issues or learning disabilities, Sally did not function as a rational, independent decision maker, according to herself and those who knew her (Mangan, 2019). It is understandable for the police to have not immediately realised this upon her arrest. However, this highlights the issues associated with assuming that our decisions are always guided by pure reason; there are other factors that may influence these. Police legitimacy can suffer if the underlying principles of RCT are unquestioningly accepted without further context.

- What are your views as to whether Sally committed murder, manslaughter or no offence at all?

- Where do your ideas come from, in terms of moral instruction?

Sample answers are provided at the end of this book.

EVIDENCE-BASED POLICING

RATIONAL CHOICE THEORY AND POLICE LEGITIMACY

It is important to understand the possible implications of principles of RCT on police legitimacy. Deterrence is a popular idea in the mainstream press and many sections of society. However, the way in which this is implemented can cause greater problems, with some sections of the community feeling they are under excessive scrutiny and surveillance. One example of this is stop and search, where officers have the power to detain (in public) individuals where there is reasonable ground for suspicion and if the legal grounds are sufficiently explained to search them for items such as stolen goods or drugs. However, researchers argue that both aspects are subjective and often poorly executed by officers, especially when young black men (in particular) are disproportionately affected and feel profiled and targeted (Bradford, 2017). Moreover, such policies are controversial because their effectiveness is hard to measure: if you are mostly stopping people who are not violating the law, is this working as a deterrent or are you harassing innocent people? If they do have illegal articles, is this a sign your intelligence is strong and an ethical, pre-emptive policy? Or has it failed as a deterrent? Such questions have implications for police legitimacy in the eyes of communities.

COMMUNITY ATTITUDES TO POLICIES UNDERPINNED BY RATIONAL CHOICE THEORY

It is important to understand that no police action takes place in a vacuum. There is always historical context which impacts how policies are perceived. RCT-influenced policies are no different. When examining how helpful they are to current officers, you must be mindful of this. The examples below will help illustrate why this is important.

POLICING SPOTLIGHT

DETECTION THROUGH CRIME CONTROL AND IT'S COMPLICATIONS

Traditionally, many sections of the community, particularly those who recall more community-based policing as a default, often eagerly embrace the idea of a 'bobby on the beat' as an ideal deterrent. However, to fulfil the requirements of SAT and RAT, the principles of RCT suggest that technological intervention may be just as effective (O'Malley and Smith, 2022). In addition to reducing the comforting, human element of policing, such changes are fraught with unintended consequences: deployment of listening devices in areas with specific racial and religious demographics has led to accusations of profiling; moreover, facial recognition technology has higher error rates when analysing the features of black citizens – this could have devastating consequences for both miscarriages of justice and public perception of policing and the criminal justice system in general (O'Malley and Smith, 2022). This casts doubt on whether simply altering an environment to introduce a deterrent or protector, in the form of a smart device, actually best serves the community.

It is important to consider if the principles of RCT do actually yield results. As discussed, the picture of a local 'bobby on the beat', who knows his (and the traditional picture featured a 'he') local area and knows residents by name, popping in for a cup of tea and reassuring chat once a week, is a popular one. However, evidence suggests that this approach has limited effectiveness in terms of crime prevention (O'Neill, 2011). This flies in the face of RCT, where the presence of a potential obstacle to offending should cause a drop in crime. Moreover, it prompts a political and ethical dilemma: Should you care more about the look and feel or the end result? Is it more important to placate our communities and comfort them or to serve most effectively? Is there a way to square this circle? And if so, how does it fit with the principles of RCT? It does not seem to fit perfectly within the logic of the theory.

The idea of RCT rests upon the idea that by simply making crime fail to pay sufficiently, individuals can be deterred from this; this seems logical and sensible. However, you have already seen a number of exceptions to this. Nevertheless, punitive punishment is very popular within the press and the police role in making it possible is seen as a core element of an effective justice system (Chong et al, 2018). Researchers also highlight links between overall satisfaction with one's life and the likelihood of offending, with those who are more content less likely to commit crime (Olson et al, 2021). This suggests that the reasons for offending may be more complex and less easily understood by someone unfamiliar with the individual than RCT might suggest.

SUMMARY

RCT is an accessible, logical theoretical paradigm which rests upon the idea that humans can make logical decisions and we can deter crime by acknowledging this. RCT and the principles associated with it have been extremely influential in England and Wales; however, these concepts have a number of critics, who highlight the limitations of these ideas, in relation to both the philosophy behind them and the effectiveness of actions taken by the criminal justice system which have been influenced by RCT.

It is for you to consider how helpful these ideas are to you in your studies and future career. You may feel this is the most logical way to look at human behaviour; or that it is unhelpful and does not understand the complexities of individuals and communities; or that it applies sometimes but there are some circumstances in which you would not apply these ideas.

REFLECTIVE PRACTICE 4.2

LEVELS 4, 5 AND 6

SCENARIO 1

You are co-ordinating a campus policing team for a local university. You have had a number of burglaries at university halls reported to you, and there is no intelligence on likely suspects. Students are increasingly concerned, and staff are asking if you can discuss a response with the students and do something to practically reduce the number of burglaries.

- What do you do?

SCENARIO 2

You are a sergeant who has been asked by your commanding officer to deal with the following: A local nightclub has complained that a young man is intimidating customers as they enter and exit the club; this has happened twice in the last week. This is the third establishment within the area to complain of similar disturbances. The man allegedly rants about a conspiracy to kidnap him, accuses some of the customers of being undercover secret service agents, and physically pushes some of them.

No one has provided a detailed description; one white woman said she thinks the man might be 'Asian or maybe black or something' but admits the street was poorly lit and she rushed past him quickly. All witnesses agree the man is tall, in a dark, hooded coat and generally covers most of his face. You attend the club and see a man who appears to be of Indian heritage extraction standing alone outside the club, in a coat with a hood. He is not speaking or moving closer to anyone. There are several white men also wearing coats with hoods; some are standing with friends, some queuing to enter the club and one is standing alone, apparently checking his phone.

- What do you do next?

Sample answers are provided at the end of this book.

REFLECTIVE PRACTICE 4.3

LEVEL 5

To further examine your own ideas, please examine the two scenarios detailed in the section above and address the following questions when considering each.

- What actions would the principles of RCT guide you towards (either RAT or SAT)?
- Why might this approach work?
- What outcome might you expect?
- Have you come across a similar scenario in real life (personally or in the media)?
- What could go wrong?
- What would the wider implications be?
- What would be an alternative?
- What would you choose to do?
- What main factors are you considering?
- How does this fit with RCT?

Sample answers are provided at the end of this book.

SUMMARY OF KEY CONCEPTS

This chapter has explored the following key concepts.

- **Rational Choice Theory:** the theory (or theories) that argues that individuals make a decision as to whether to offend or not based on the likely outcome (Thomas et al, 2020).

- **Utilitarianism:** the idea that you act to maximise your pleasure and minimise your pain; it is moral to aim for the greatest pleasure for the greatest number of people (Bentham, 1983).

- **Deterrence:** the idea that if you want something but the punishment for doing it is too severe, you will not attempt it; you will be deterred.

- **Routine Activity Theory:** the theory that crime occurs when three specific factors unite: (1) a motivated offender; (2) a suitable target (or victim); (3) the absence of a capable guardian (Cohen and Felson, 1979).

- **Situational Action Theory:** the theory that is also part of RCT criminology, which assumes that (1) people are basically guided by rules, and you express your wants and respond to stress in this context; (2) social order is based on norms that are mutually agreed social rules which guide routines and social behaviour; (3) people generate their own actions – they make choices and carry these out; (4) actions differ depending on the situation: the context influences perception of the available options, the process of choosing from these and how you perform them and you interact with your environment to make a decision; and (5) crimes are moral actions which contravene the law, which guides us as to right or wrong in that context (Wikström and Treiber, 2018).

CHECK YOUR KNOWLEDGE

1. What would a utilitarian argue is the purpose of the police?

2. What deterrents in your life have prevented you from offending when you could have gained something by doing so?

3. How can utilitarianism be applied to demands for a greater focus on community policing?

4. Can you think of a circumstance in which the fear of getting caught is less important than the potential pleasure provided by offending?

5. What factors prevented Bentley from being able to rationalise?

6. What factors can limit a person's ability to think logically? How might you, as an officer, need to account for these?

7. What do you think about stop and search?

Sample answers are provided at the end of this book.

FURTHER READING

These resources will help you to enhance your understanding of the subjects covered in the chapter.

Beccaria, C (1995) *Beccaria: 'On Crimes and Punishments' and Other Writings*. Cambridge: Cambridge University Press.

Becker, G S (1968) Crime and Punishment: An Economic Analysis. *Journal of Political Economy*, 78: 169–217.

Bentham, J (1983) *The Collected Works of Jeremy Bentham: Deontology. Together with a Table of the Springs of Action and the Article on Utilitarianism*. Oxford: Clarendon Press.

Cohen, L E and Felson M (1979) Social Change and Crime Rate Trends: A Routine Activity Approach. *American Sociological Review*, 44: 588–605.

Cornish, D and Clarke, R (1987) Understanding Crime Displacement: An Application of Rational Choice Theory. *Criminology*, 25(4): 933–47.

Hayward, K (2007) Situational Crime Prevention and Its Discontents: Rational Choice Theory versus the 'Culture of Now'. *Social Policy & Administration*, 41(3): 232–50.

CHAPTER 5
SITUATIONAL CRIME PREVENTION

LEARNING OBJECTIVES

AFTER READING THIS CHAPTER YOU WILL BE ABLE TO:

- understand the term crime prevention and associated methods and strategies that seek to reduce the chances of crime occurring;

- offer practical advice and guidance linked to a range of crime prevention measures;

- apply situational crime prevention initiatives to a range of relevant scenarios, both from a policing perspective and to wider society;

- identify what makes an item or product 'hot' and what this means to both the offender and the police;

- understand the concept of Crime Prevention Through Environmental Design (CPTED) and how the built environment can positively reduce the chances of crime occurring;

- critically evaluate the ethical implications associated with situational crime prevention.

INTRODUCTION

> *Crime destroys lives. Victims are often left traumatised, injured or heartbroken. Crime can ruin neighbourhoods and does great damage to our country. It makes people feel unsafe on the street and in their homes. Criminal activity fuels and funds huge criminal enterprises. Involvement in crime can set someone on a path that brings enormous harm to themselves and others.*
>
> (Beating Crime Plan, Gov.uk, 2021, p 3)

Having property stolen or damaged or being victim of a crime such as burglary can have a major impact on an individual, family or business, and so it is understandable that we take relevant steps to protect our homes and belongings from those with criminal intentions. Within your career as a police officer, you will often be the first port of call for people who have suffered a traumatic experience such as this. You will be expected to not only provide support for the victim but be part of the investigatory process and bring about a swift resolution.

It makes good sense that all newly recruited officers have a comprehensive understanding of crime prevention and the ability to offer sensible and attainable measures that people, businesses and organisations can apply to their daily lives and working routines.

This chapter explores the concept of situational crime prevention (deterring crime by making changes to the environment), encompassing broader crime prevention initiatives and strategies. It encourages you to think about measures that you can implement to not only protect your home and belongings, but which also underpin a range of practical crime prevention advice that you can carry forward to your policing role in the future.

The concluding section of the chapter asks you to consider the ethical implications associated with situational crime prevention and the use of surveillance technology, encouraging you to think about what it may mean from a practical policing standpoint and more broadly for the future of policing.

CRIME PREVENTION

Historically, crime prevention in Britain was predominantly considered to be the responsibility of the police (Walklate, 2013, cited in McLaughlin and Muncie, 2013) and this attitude still clearly exists within modern policing today. This is evidenced not just via police–community interactions but through organisations with dedicated crime prevention officers/crime prevention teams or indeed via webpages dedicated to crime prevention advice. However, it is worth noting that the police's approach to crime prevention has changed over time, with less emphasis given to crime prevention and more focus placed on more pressing, intensive and resource-heavy policework.

As explored by Tilley (2009), other related phrases such as 'crime reduction', 'public safety' and 'community safety' have been used at various times and have clear links to the overarching theme of crime prevention, though they also incorporate the fear of being involved in crime and risk to a person, which has a slightly different leaning and will not be explored within this chapter.

Simply put, crime prevention comprises a range of strategies and initiatives with the goal of reducing the chance of crime to occur. This can be achieved through private enterprise, state policies and involvement with the law (Hughes, 1998), as well as common-sense methods that seek to reduce vulnerability and mitigate weaknesses.

In the early 1980s, the Conservative government proposed reform that explored crime prevention from a community-based perspective, recognising that engagement from local communities alongside partnership agencies and the police would offer the best combination in tackling the associated challenges of crime prevention. It was felt that two main assumptions of crime prevention could be further explored and understood to gain a better overview of how to implement measures under the umbrella of crime prevention.

1. To gain an understanding of the causes of crime and therefore how it might be prevented.

2. To understand the nature of communities and the impact they could have in matters of crime prevention.

On their own, both assumptions will go a long way to address some of the fundamental issues surrounding crime prevention – for example, taking steps to safeguard a property or business – but combined they offer a two-pronged approach, giving the greatest chance of success and the best way of implementing change.

CRITICAL THINKING ACTIVITY 5.1

LEVEL 4

Why is crime prevention needed? Take your time to consider this question. If it was an essay question, how would you go about answering it?

A sample answer is provided at the end of this book.

25 TECHNIQUES OF CRIME PREVENTION

Cornish and Clarke (2003) developed a practical and useable table that incorporated 25 techniques of situational crime prevention, which detailed various types of interventions that people and organisations could use to reduce crime. The 25 techniques were split into five specific groups, as detailed below with a brief overview of each category.

1. Increase the effort

The objective of this category is to make it more difficult for the offender to be able to carry out their task – hence a greater effort on their part will be needed. This could include relatively simple measures such as adding steering wheel/disk locks to cars or motorbikes, or disabling mobile phones once they are reported as stolen.

2. Increase the risk

These measures aim to increase the risk to offenders (chances of them being caught) in the hope that they will be deterred from carrying out any form of criminal act. In this category, measures such as an increased use of CCTV cameras, greater number of staff members working in a shop or the addition of burglar alarms should act as enough of a deterrent to deter most offenders.

3. Reduce the rewards

The premise of this category is to limit the rewards available to the offender by making items either difficult to locate or difficult to access. For example, ensuring that all valuables have been removed from a car such as expensive audio equipment, laptop bags and mobile phones should suggest that a particular vehicle will no longer be a viable target as there is nothing to be gained from breaking into it. Other measures such as close monitoring of local pawn shops and cash-converting businesses should restrict the sale of stolen items.

4. Reduce provocations

Here it is important to adjust areas that could cause provocations – in essence, something that causes annoyance or frustration and will likely end in some form of unwanted action such as verbal abuse or physical assault. This category includes measures such as keeping rival supporters separate at sporting events, fixing prices for taxi fares prior to the journey beginning and fast-moving queues to limit aggravation.

5. Remove excuses

The measures in the final category place the emphasis on individuals, businesses and organisations to take steps to reduce the chance for 'excuses' to be used. For example, electronic speed signs that display current speeds (usually combined with happy/sad faces depending on speed) are hard for drivers to ignore and it is hoped they will therefore regulate their speed accordingly. Other simple steps could be to add more litter bins in areas that have problems with littering and better signage, providing simple instructions for people to follow.

Table 5.1 Cornish and Clarke's 25 techniques of crime prevention

Increase the effort	Increase the risk	Reduce the rewards	Reduce provocations	Remove excuses
1. Target hardening Steering column locks Tamper-proof packaging	**6. Extend guardianship** Take precautions – go out in groups, leave lights on, carry a mobile phone Join Neighbourhood Watch groups	**11. Conceal targets** Use off-street parking facilities Gender-neutral phone book	**16. Reduce frustrations and stress** Polite services and quick-moving queues Increase seating	**21. Set rules** Rental agreements Hotel registrations
2. Control access to facilities Electronic card access Entry phones	**7. Assist natural surveillance** Improved street lighting Support whistle-blowers	**12. Remove targets** Removable car audio Women's refuges	**17. Avoid disputes** Fixed taxi prices Separate rival football supporters	**22. Post instructions** 'Private property' 'No parking'
3. Screen exits Tickets needed for exit Electronic merchandise tags	**8. Reduce anonymity** Taxi driver IDs School/work uniforms	**13. Identity property** Property marking Vehicle registrations	**18. Reduce emotional arousal** Control on violent pornography Enforce good behaviour at sporting events	**23. Alert conscience** Roadside speed signs – happy/unhappy faces 'Shoplifting is theft'

Table 5.1 (continued)

Increase the effort	Increase the risk	Reduce the rewards	Reduce provocations	Remove excuses
4. Deflect offenders Disperse pubs Street closures	**9. Utilise place managers** Reward vigilance CCTV cameras on buses	**14. Disrupt markets** Monitor pawn shops/cash converters License street vendors	**19. Neutralise peer pressure** Disperse troublemakers from school environment Drink and drive campaigns	**24. Assist compliance** Litter bins readily available Public lavatories
5. Control tools/ weapons Age restrictions on spray cans Disable stolen mobile phones	**10. Strengthen formal surveillance** Burglar alarms Red light cameras	**15. Deny benefits** Add speed bumps Graffiti cleaning	**20. Discourage imitation** Rapid repair of vandalism Content control of internet/TV sources	**25. Control drugs and alcohol** Alcohol-free events Server interventions

Adapted from Cornish and Clarke (2003)

As shown in Table 5.1, Cornish and Clarke's (2003) grid offers a range of relevant measures and interventions that can be applied in a variety of scenarios to reduce the chance of criminal actions taking place, offering sound practical guidance that can be used in your role as a police officer.

That said, the table was devised roughly 20 years ago and while the content is still incredibly relevant and applicable to modern society, it is to be expected that new ways of tackling crime, combined with the development of new technology, may offer other methods that would situate themselves well within the table.

REFLECTIVE PRACTICE 5.1

LEVEL 6

- Take some time to consider each of the sections in the table and refresh your understanding of the five categories.

1. Increase the effort

2. Increase the risk

3. Reduce the rewards

4. Reduce provocations

5. Remove excuses

- Then suggest a range of additional measures that you could implement and place your ideas into the relevant boxes. For example, you may want to consider relevant technology such as smart doorbells and the potential they have to positively impact home security and offer homeowners a sense of security both in and away from their properties.

- Try and draw from a combination of personal experience and what you may have seen and read about, developing both your research skills and practical application of ideas.

- Can you come up with an example for each of the 25 boxes?

- Are there any other categories that you feel are missing? If so, what are they and justify why they should be included.

Sample answers are provided at the end of this book.

THE 'HOT' MODEL OF CRIME

Drawing from the work of Clarke (1999), Bryant and Bryant (2019) refer to a number of key components (with a particular emphasis on stolen goods) of crime that occur with regular frequency and, as such, are directly linked to crime and criminality and should be at the forefront of most operational officers' minds.

HOT SPOTS

Largely understood to be places that are especially vulnerable to crime (Braga and Weisburd, 2010), 'hot spots' could include shopping centres, railways stations and town centres to name but a few. They naturally become areas of interest to criminals as the sheer volume of people who will transit through the areas will be high, and so they offer relatively easy pickings for people intent on committing crimes such as theft or shoplifting. Features such as access to large quantities of desirable items, cash machines and people carrying expensive products ensure that opportunities to commit crime remain possible and can therefore be exploited by the criminally minded accordingly. Due to scenarios such as this, there was an obvious need for the police to develop a practical method of tackling the policing of hot spot areas, hence the evolution of the hot spot policing model as a strategy for crime prevention.

CRITICAL THINKING ACTIVITY 5.2

HOT SPOT POLICING

Lazzati and Menichini (2016, p 893) define hot spot policing as, '*a place-based strategy that attempts to reduce crime by assigning limited police resources to places where crimes are more highly concentrated*'.

LEVEL 4

- Using the definition above as a guideline, develop your own interpretation of hot spot policing that would help you explain the concept to one of your peers (with no police knowledge).

LEVEL 5

- Carry out your own research into hot spot policing as a model to tackle criminal behaviour and consider if there are any other policing models that can be used in conjunction to aid the police in their task.

LEVEL 6

- Undertake further reading into hot spot policing and critically review the framework as a model to tackle criminal behaviour. What are the strengths and limitations of the model? Are there better policing models out there that could achieve the same goal?

LEVELS 4, 5 AND 6

Apply the hot spot policing model to the following scenarios and explore the effectiveness at each stage:

- a busy railway station in a major city such as Manchester, Birmingham or London;

- a block of flats in an economically deprived area;

- a university campus;

- a popular high street with several pubs, bars and nightclubs along it.

Sample answers are provided at the end of this book.

HOT VICTIMS

The term 'ideal victim' was brought into the mainstream by leading sociologist and criminologist Nils Christie in 1986 (Duggan, 2018), developing the earlier work of Von Hentig (1948) and Mendelsohn (1976), and describes both the features/characteristics of the victim and the activities they were engaged in. Briefly put, Christie's theory consists of five attributes that help you to produce a visual representation of the ideal victim. The ideal victim would:

- be weak (*child/elderly/disabled*);

- be engaged in a respectable activity (*visiting a friend in hospital/going to church*);

- be involved in a respectable activity that would take part at a reasonable time (*midday not 3am*);

- be subject to attack from someone menacing (*a 'big' 'bad' man with tattoos who robs people to buy drugs*);

- have no relationship with the offender (*not someone they know and is more a meeting by chance*).

The 'hot victim' description aligns closely with Christie's work – many of the same ideas exist of which type of people are likely to be targeted, though in reality a 'hot victim' could be any person on the street. The one exception to the rule is for the offence of 'distraction burglary' where an offender gains access into the property of an elderly or vulnerable person under the guise of being an official. An example of this could be someone who enters a property on the pretence of reading a gas or electricity meter, but instead steals items and belongings from within.

See the link within the further reading section to explore more of Christie's ideal victim theory.

HOT OFFENDERS

The third element of the hot model is simplistic and focuses on 'hot offenders', recognising that it is a relatively small number of people who are responsible for a large proportion of crime. Some offenders will favour certain types of crime such as those who are attracted to the excitement and rewards to be gained from committing burglary, while others prefer acting by chance and are far more opportunistic. What is worth noting here is that within your role as a police officer and as someone who offers preventative advice, in many cases the same individual may be subject to the same type of crime and become a repeat victim. This is commonly seen in cases such as domestic violence, as well as burglaries where an offender has been successful and chooses to go back for more; therefore, the way you deal with repeat victims may need a different approach.

HOT PRODUCTS

The final element of the 'hot' model of crime as developed by Bryant and Bryant (2019), with acknowledgement of the work of Clarke (1999), discusses the term 'hot products'. These are described as items that are more attractive to burglars, thieves and street robbers; deciding which items to steal involves some logic on the part of the offender. The most frequently targeted items are relatively small, easily movable or hard to trace – in particular, items such as cash, mobile phones and jewellery are top of this list of items to be stolen.

CRITICAL THINKING ACTIVITY 5.3

LEVEL 4

NEIGHBOURHOOD POLICING

As a newly appointed police constable working within your local neighbourhood policing team, you have been tasked by your supervisor to develop a list of 'hot product' items that will eventually form a poster to be distributed around your local area. The poster should inform people of some of the main items that will fall into the hot products category, as well as offering some basic advice on how people can better protect their belongings. The poster will be displayed in a range of locations such as schools, shops, businesses, community centres and places of worship, so needs to be accessible for all ages.

- Take some time to consider items that may fall within the hot products category – consider items that are easy to sell on, have a high resale value or are on trend and desirable.

- What suggestions would you make to people within your neighbourhood on how they could best protect these items?

- What challenges will the police face from the theft of hot product items?

Sample answers are provided at the end of this book.

CRAVED

When considering hot products and desirable items, it is worthwhile utilising the mnemonic CRAVED as a way of remembering what makes an item more at risk of being stolen. This phrase will work as a great aid in your future role as a police officer, allowing you to share your knowledge with members of the public while giving them some simple steps to implement to reduce the risk of theft.

C	Concealable	Items that you would naturally place in pockets or bags are at greater risk of being targeted by sneak thieves and shoplifters. Not only are these types of items easily concealable by the offender, but they are difficult to identify once they have been stolen.
R	Removable	Items that are mobile by design such as bikes and cars – plus more on-trend modes of transport such as e-scooters – explains why they are so often stolen as they offer a means for a quick exit. Other items such as laptops in bags, rucksacks and handbags are also easy targets as they can be grabbed because they usually have handles designed to aid carrying.
A	Available	Readily available and attractive items will always be at higher risk, hence the reason why households tend to make more of a concerted effort to hide jewellery and cash. Crime trends also tend to follow the establishment of new hot products – the introduction of the mobile phone into the mainstream in the 1990s is an excellent example of this and can establish its own illegal market.
V	Valuable	Expensive items and goods will regularly be targeted by thieves, particularly when their intention is to sell the item on to make money. That said, not all items that can be classed as valuable have a high monetary value; indeed, some items are stolen as they may offer status among their peers (for example, a high-performing car).
E	Enjoyable	The enjoyment that can be derived from stealing a particular item and the use of the item itself may be at the forefront of the decision to commit theft. Items such as computer games, alcohol and cigarettes are all common items that are stolen and may offer the thief pleasure and enjoyment over and above simply stealing for financial gain.

D Disposable   Many thieves will target items that can be easily sold on and can be out of their possession relatively quickly. Among other items, products such as batteries and razor blades are regularly taken from shops as they are both small in size and so easily pocketable, and in demand so could be exchanged for cash or drugs.

From a practical policing perspective, it is important to understand that while the CRAVED model is being applied to crime prevention initiatives in this section, it has far-reaching connotations and can be applied to a different range of criminality such as sexual homicide (Beauregard and Martineau, 2015). See the link within the further reading section to explore further applications of the CRAVED model.

EVIDENCE-BASED POLICING

CHANGING MARKETS

It has been well documented that the recent global pandemic impacted the world, and one outcome was that people's behaviours were influenced (Regalado et al, 2022), in particular in the world of crime and deviance. The enforced Covid-19 lockdown(s) saw a decline in certain crime types such as assault, robbery and theft, though there was an increase in other notable areas such as violent behaviours and cybercrime.

During the Covid-19 lockdowns, various markets rapidly began to change, shift and adapt to keep pace with the requirements of the country and the movement restrictions that were placed on all, with delivery drivers swiftly becoming national heroes alongside NHS workers. For example, reported figures (Harris, 2020) suggested that Amazon doubled its quarterly profits during lockdown and while this invariably made its owners and shareholders wealthier, the service they provided to members across the globe was arguably one of importance in incredibly challenging circumstances. Like Amazon, other delivery markets saw a noticeable boom both within the fast-food sector, as well as in other sectors such as household items and pharmaceutical products. Of note was the pet ownership market with figures from BBC News (2021) suggesting that households purchased 3.2 million pets during lockdown – this was a reported rise of around 11 per cent (Statista, 2022b) for dogs alone between 2019/20 and 2021/22.

As with most markets, the unprecedented demand for pets during lockdown meant an increase in the cost of animals and the price of puppies, where most (if not all) breeds doubled in price. Due to the increase in both pet sales and pet prices, it was not surprising to see (though unexpected) that dog thefts rose by 25 per cent between 2021 and 2022 (Crimestoppers, 2023) with up to five pets being stolen per day. With an average price of approximately £1900 per dog, this example serves to highlight how a market can suddenly boom, the value assigned to each item can soar and how a product can become increasingly more desirable – the CRAVED mnemonic can certainly be applied here.

REFLECTIVE PRACTICE 5.2

LEVEL 4

While studying on a professional policing programme or similar degree, there is scope to actively engage with crime fighting and crime resolution through voluntary positions within the police, such as becoming a special constable and working for organisations such as Crimestoppers and Victim Support. For some of you, working as a special constable may not be an option, but it is worth considering other forms of community engagement where you can play your part and make a difference to your neighbourhoods. Schemes such as Neighbourhood Watch (www.ourwatch.org.uk) (see Neighbourhood Watch, 2020), whose focus is on building community groups and reducing burglaries and other home and personal crimes, have been in existence since the early 1980s and have a strong working relationship with their local forces. While initially their focus was on the protection of homes and property, their scope has diversified and they regularly recruit for cyber and hate crime ambassadors, alongside community champions who offer situational crime prevention advice on areas such as burglary, car crime and bicycle theft.

Other opportunities to support community-led projects include schemes such as the West Mercia Police and West Midlands Police 'Street Watch' scheme, where groups go out on patrol within their local communities with the intention to report any criminal or anti-social behaviour to the police and help build community relationships. The Metropolitan Police (2022) recruit Community Based Volunteers (CBVs) who assist the police with events in their neighbourhoods, such as night-time patrols that may support vulnerable people walking home on their own, alongside other crime prevention initiatives such as bike marking and crime prevention events. This demonstrates a range of practical initiatives that anyone who is passionate about the protection of their neighbourhood and communities can become involved with and draw clear links to situational and crime prevention initiatives without having to be in a position as a police officer or police staff member.

- What voluntary positions are there within your local force area that you could become involved with?

- Consider joining your local Facebook and WhatsApp neighbourhood groups – they can be a great source of information and allow you to engage with like-minded community-conscious people.

- Follow your local Neighbourhood Policing Unit on Twitter – regular posts and updates will again offer practical advice on crime prevention initiatives and measures that you can share with your friends and families.

- How would you convince others to actively engage with schemes such as the ones above?

SITUATIONAL CRIME PREVENTION

As defined by the College of Policing (2022, p 1), situational crime prevention *'focuses on the settings where crime occurs, rather than on those committing specific criminal acts'* and explores the need to make both environmental and managerial changes that help reduce criminal opportunities. Situational crime prevention has close links with two criminological theories, as explored in Chapter 4:

1. Rational Choice Theory (RCT);

2. Routine Activity Theory (RAT).

The overarching goal of situational crime prevention is to make the opportunity for committing the act either too difficult (increasing the risk of the offender being caught) or with low reward (not worth the risk to the offender) to reduce levels of criminality.

Tilley (2009, p 105) further explores situational crime prevention in practice, recognising the need to *'find ways of reducing crime problems by reducing or removing opportunities'* with an onus on where the current preventative measures do not appear to be robust or adequate enough and therefore warrant further investigation. It is worth noting at this point that situational crime prevention measures can be applied to a wide range of areas of criminality such as sexual offences against women (Chiu et al, 2021), violent crimes in educational settings (Sevigny and Zhang, 2018) and organised crime (von Lampe, 2011) among others, though for the purpose of this chapter the focus will be more on 'low levels' of criminality.

As previously stated, one of the purposes of situational crime prevention is to pay close attention to the settings where crime occurs and devise measures of reducing criminal acts, rather than trying to highlight and arrest people involved with carrying out the act. Therefore, the emphasis is on the development of ideas and products to support individuals and businesses to protect their assets. This can be examined using the example of theft of high-value fashion items from within a designer shop and measures that can be implemented to make this far more challenging to someone looking to steal.

- To prevent a number of similar items (for example, jackets) from being stolen from a clothes rail, staff can alternate the direction the hangers are placed on the rail, making it more difficult for a number of jackets to be swept up in one motion. This serves two main purposes – (1) if the thief is unaware of the hanger positions and tries to take lots of jackets in one go, the hangers should make a good deal of noise that will alert staff members to the area; (2) if the thief is aware of the hanger positioning and decides to take the jackets off their hangers first, it will take additional time to remove them, meaning they will need to spend more time in the area which may raise suspicion.

- Security tags and dye tags can be fitted to products (particularly those of highest value or the most stolen), which will sound an alarm on exit and alert staff members. Dye tags, if removed incorrectly, have the capacity to stain the garment, thus reducing its value and highlighting to potential purchasers that it was likely stolen.

- Businesses place items of greatest value closest to areas where staff are situated such as tills and pay points. This increases the risk of an offender being spotted and may discourage them from attempting to steal as staff members may be on high alert in these areas. In addition, security staff, whether in uniform or plain clothes, may spend more time patrolling and surveilling these areas to minimise risk of theft.

What is important to note from the example above is that some of the suggested measures to reduce crime are relatively simplistic and cheap to implement. From a practical perspective, one of the fundamental ideas surrounding situational crime prevention is that there needs to be a degree of pragmatism that can be applied to the steps to follow or take and, for all but large organisations with deep pockets, cost needs to be a driving factor. While there is a cost for purchasing features such as security and dye tags, plus the technology needed to use them in a practical setting, they are designed to be used repeatedly – thus offsetting some of the initial cost.

CRITICAL THINKING ACTIVITY 5.4

LEVEL 5

Assuming the role of a crime prevention officer, produce a range of practical crime reduction strategies that can be implemented within the settings listed below. Within your rationale, include recommendations that are low cost and quick to implement, plus others that may require a greater financial outlay and therefore greater investment by the owner or organisation.

- A bike shop within a busy town centre.

- A community centre with both indoor and outdoor activities.

- A large department store split over three floors.

- An out-of-town car dealership.

- A small convenience store, close to a busy railway station.

Sample answers are provided at the end of this book.

CRIME PREVENTION THROUGH ENVIRONMENTAL DESIGN

The concept of Crime Prevention Through Environmental Design (CPTED) is not a new one – in essence, this has been seen throughout human history and can span as far back as early cave dwellers, where prehistoric man would have chosen caves to live in that offered them shelter and security, as well as likely being close to water and food resources. Fast forward thousands of years and similar decisions can be seen to be made by kings and queens of old; the placement of a castle on top of a hill was a well-considered approach – it offered great visibility, made it difficult for approaching armies to access, had thick, strong walls that were difficult to break through, and gates that would be securely locked and manned, restricting the access of unwanted visitors.

More recently, CPTED strategies can be seen throughout the modern world and will naturally form part of the planning and design phases of architects and town planners. The way buildings are constructed, spaces are lit, roads are built, hedges are planted and CCTV is installed all serve to reduce the chances of criminal acts occurring. CPTED should be seen as a problem-solving approach that seeks to utilise the environment to control access, provide opportunities to see and be seen and define ownership and maintenance of an area (Zahm, 2007). In doing so, the opportunities for undesirable behaviour and criminality should be lessened, leaving neighbourhoods safer and improving the quality of life for inhabitants.

In its current guise, CPTED has been recognised as both an academic discipline as well as comprising a set of practical guidelines for reducing the opportunity for criminal activity; it is based on several studies conducted since the 1960s (Cozens et al, 2005). The underlying principles of CPTED loosely fall within six core categories or characteristics (Moffat, 1983) though there is a good deal of scope for overlap of each category as they are undoubtedly closely linked.

1. **Territoriality** – the concept of territoriality and territorial reinforcement includes the design elements of landscaping, paths and pavements, as well as structures such as porches on the front of a building to differentiate between public and private areas. Here, a sense of ownership is applied (Cozens et al, 2005), suggesting that they will be used for legitimate means and discourage people from abusing the areas.

2. **Surveillance (formal and informal)**

    a) **Formal** – CCTV cameras are an excellent example of formal surveillance, having been installed for a purpose (usually a deterrent) and can assist with police investigations if needed. Other forms of formal surveillance could be security staff in shops, car park attendants and hotel doormen, who offer a physical presence to deter potential offenders, as well as police officers on patrol.

    b) **Informal** – informal surveillance can include elements such as quality lighting along a street and the placement of windows at the front of a property looking out to the road, which gives potential offenders the assumption that they are being watched from within and therefore they are less likely to commit any unwanted acts.

3. **Access control** – elements that are seen in nature such as shrubs, bushes and hedges can form a natural access control point and when combined with man-made structures such as gates, fencing and doors they serve a purpose to restrict people's movements (Badiora and Adebara, 2020). This then creates an increased awareness of risk in the mind of the offender, which may cause them to reconsider their willingness to commit crime.

4. **Image/maintenance** – it is important that due care and attention is paid to a particular space and that regular maintenance allows for the space to be used

for its intended purposes. An area that is allowed to fall into disrepair may not only become a risk to public health and safety but be subject to concepts such as Broken Windows Theory (see below) and be at greater risk of being negatively exploited.

5. **Activity support** – this aspect explores the idea of placing 'unsafe' activities in 'safe' locations. An example of this is the placement of cash machines in areas that are well lit and with high footfall, the idea being that there should be a good number of pedestrians walking by who act as natural surveillance and should discourage offenders from taking action. In reality, this does not necessarily apply, as higher foot traffic means chances for pickpockets and sneak thieves to strike.

6. **Target hardening** – this is a traditional approach to crime prevention and focuses on the use of additional measures to add extra layers of security to a property (gates, fences, barriers, alarms, locks and security staff) that increase the amount of effort an offender must expend to commit the crime. The use of target-hardening measures conflicts with much of the CPTED concept, and switches from using the natural and built environment (combined with smart design ideas) to deter criminal behaviours to instead creating more of a fortress mentality.

BROKEN WINDOWS THEORY

Broken Windows Theory is a widely recognised and cited aspect of contemporary criminology that has clear and distinct links to policing. Early work by Wilson and Kelling at the start of the 1980s, plus additional developments since then (for example, see Welch et al, 2015), highlight how the concept has grown over time as traditionally the police would predominantly focus on serious crimes (murder, rape and robbery) as they had the greatest consequences for the victim. Eventually, the police gained a greater understanding of how communities could spiral into disorder if areas were deemed to be unsafe, with the associated knock-on effects, and they took steps to develop strategies and initiatives to rectify the problems.

The term 'broken windows' paints a visual representation of the focus of the theory, suggesting that buildings with broken windows in a given neighbourhood are more likely to descend into disorder and criminality (McLaughlin, 2019, cited in McLaughlin and Muncie, 2019) if maintenance and repair of the broken window is slow to materialise. The assumption is that both law-abiding citizens and criminals will perceive that no one cares about the building, and before too long other windows will become smashed, eventually causing a ripple effect that compromises community safety and the upkeep of a neighbourhood, paving the way for more serious levels of criminality. The stages of Broken Windows Theory are illustrated in Figure 5.1.

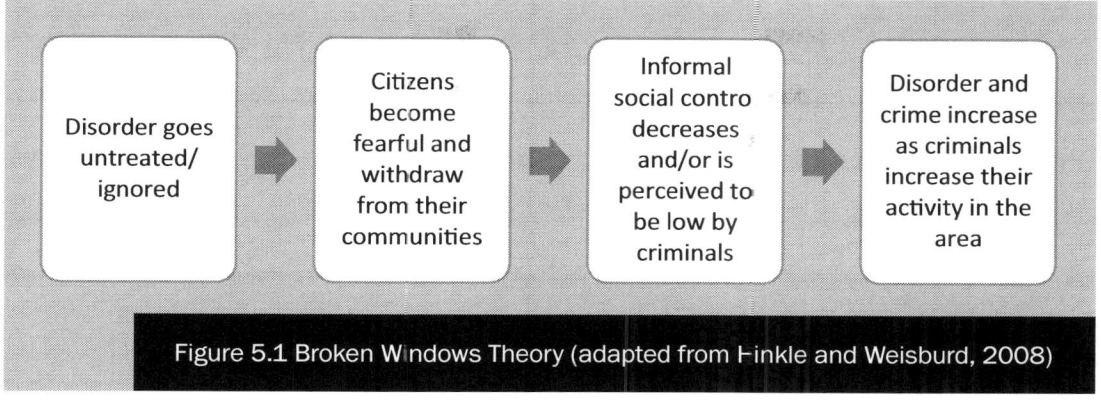

Figure 5.1 Broken Windows Theory (adapted from Hinkle and Weisburd, 2008)

From a practical policing perspective, Broken Windows Theory goes further than simple damage to a building to explore other criminal acts and behaviours that may become commonplace, such as vandalism, loitering, public consumption of alcohol, evidence of drug dealing, prostitution and the creation of an environment that fosters even more crime and disorder.

POLICING SPOTLIGHT

CASE STUDY 1

The back wall of an office building within a business centre is repeatedly subject to being tagged with graffiti and is causing the office owner frustration and cost in cleaning it up.

WHY IS IT BEING TARGETED?

The area has been selected as it is out of view to passers-by, so the chance of being seen is low – it is a corner location where two buildings come together and is at the end of a lane that is poorly lit. Metal fencing and hedges around the perimeter further reduce visibility. The building is situated on an industrial estate where the main business hours are 0800–1800 during the week, though there is a leisure complex next door which houses arcade machines, pool tables and a bowling alley, and where activity is at its peak in the evenings and weekends.

CASE STUDY 2

Janitorial staff in a local high school regularly find evidence of smoking, drinking and vandalism in and around the external toilet block.

WHY IS IT BEING TARGETED?

The toilet block is in an isolated area of the school and away from the main teaching rooms. It is utilised most frequently by students during break times and lunch periods. Next to the toilet block is seating for sporting events, plus some tables and chairs, which give students a place to eat their snacks and lunches, relatively unobserved by staff members.

REFLECTIVE PRACTICE 5.3

LEVEL 5

Using CPTED, consider how you would tackle the challenges faced in both case studies stated in the previous policing spotlight section.

- What measures would you implement?

- What resources would you need?

- If there are costs associated with your ideas, are they reasonable and likely to be applied?

- Final thought: could your defences be defeated?

Sample answers are provided at the end of this book.

DESIGNING OUT CRIME

Another interesting concept that promotes personal safety and protection of property is the market that focuses on designing and creating products that fight back against crime. At a national level, this could be seen within the security features of a passport (Thales, 2022), the creation of bank notes and coins which make it almost impossible to produce forgeries, together with more low-cost practical ideas such as theftproof rucksacks with zippers at the back and wallets with radio-frequency identification (RFID) blocking material to stop card scanners accessing bank card information. Within your role as a police officer of the future, it is worth understanding some of the products and technology that exist in the market; you will be able to offer safety advice and make recommendations to people within your community and this will be a great way to proactively apply your knowledge.

The list below provides several examples of accessible products and technology that have been designed to deter crime:

- rucksacks;
- wallets;
- Faraday pouch/bag;
- mobile phones with biometric scanners;
- smart doorbells;
- personal safety alarms;
- dash cams;
- GPS trackers;
- various mobile phone safety applications (Hollie Guard personal safety app);
- smart lighting;
- jewellery with integrated safety features such as the Invisawear necklace with panic button.

CRITICAL THINKING ACTIVITY 5.5

LEVEL 6

Alongside the suggestions above, are there any other product/items with specific safety features built within them that you either own, have seen or have heard about?

> - What are the merits and limitations of each product?
>
> - If you had to recommend three of the products to family members and friends, which would you opt for?
>
> - What are the reasons for your choices?
>
> - Do you feel the police should work more in partnership with product designers and inventors? Don't forget to justify your answers.
>
> See the link within the further reading section to explore the development of creative solutions to design out crime and other related problems.

ETHICAL IMPLICATIONS OF SITUATIONAL CRIME PREVENTION

In a more modern age, organisations, businesses and individuals recognise the need to make use of relevant technology to support their efforts in protecting their belongings and assets, with systems such as CCTV being one of the most widespread and easily recognised methods. Goold (2004) and McCahill (2002) wrote extensively on the inclusion of CCTV cameras in most major cities in the UK from the early 1990s and the rapid expansion of the technology as a true asset to the police in their attempt to tackle widespread criminality. Since then, the number of CCTV cameras operating in the UK has grown exponentially.

From a policing, law enforcement and intelligence agency perspective, the need to carry out surveillance that encompasses those going about their daily lives is sadly a necessity to protect our country and its inhabitants. Major incidents across the globe such as 9/11 and the 7/7 bombings have highlighted the increased potential for terror attacks to take place and in doing so, has increased the need for greater surveillance and monitoring. A consequence of this however, is the often-fraught relationship that has developed between surveillance and society and will likely remain a contentious subject. Policing and law enforcement agencies need to keep pace with changing times and ensure that their technological capabilities are robust enough to tackle the demands of modern crime while recognising that the intrusive nature of situational crime preventative measures and other formal surveillance methods will be met with some resistance from society.

The Project Champion case study of 2010 serves as a great example of how a strong policing initiative by West Midlands Police Counter Terrorism Unit in 2007, when the country was in a state of high alert due to several thwarted attacks, eventually snowballed out of control and blurred the lines between proactive policing and almost total surveillance of a relatively small section of the population. Here, the proposal to include 46 new CCTV cameras and 170 ANPR cameras (some overt, some covert) came with good intentions – West Midlands Police wanted to monitor and record the movements of individuals suspected to be involved with terrorism without having to physically follow them in and out of the area. In reality, the operation breached reasonable ethical and legitimate boundaries as it ring-fenced a largely Muslim population in Birmingham, ultimately putting everyone in the area under the watch of the police. Project Champion was halted in July 2010.

CRITICAL THINKING ACTIVITY 5.6

LEVEL 5

Looking at Table 5.2, consider the associated strengths and limitations of different surveillance technologies that could be used as a range of practical situational crime prevention measures. Write down as many strengths and limitations as you can. Add any other technology types you know about to the list.

Table 5.2 Surveillance technology strengths and weaknesses

Technology	Strengths	Weaknesses
CCTV cameras (town centre)		
CCTV cameras (home owned)		
ANPR cameras (static)		
ANPR cameras (in vehicles)		
Smart phones		
Smart doorbells		
Drones		
Vehicle webcams		

- What are the ethical implications associated with these types of technology?

- What does this mean for the future of policing?

→

- In your opinion, do the positives that can be derived from surveillance technology outweigh the negatives? Ensure you justify your answers.

- Read the 2010 Project Champion Review by Thames Valley Police (link in the further reading section) and offer a critique of the proposal. At which point do you feel the operation broke ethical practices and why? If you oversaw the operation, what would you have done differently to ensure it was successful and not met with such fierce opposition from the local community?

SUMMARY OF KEY CONCEPTS

This chapter has explored the following key concepts.

- Crime prevention, although important to the police, is often overshadowed by more pressing, comprehensive and resource-heavy crimes.

- Crime prevention is most successful with the engagement of both the police and the community.

- Situational crime prevention focuses on making changes to the environment to reduce the chances of crime occurring, looking at *how* crime happens and not *why* it happens.

- Situational crime prevention measures encompass a range of simplistic, pragmatic and technological solutions to reduce the chance of crime occurring.

- CPTED is an important process in protecting and securing our homes, streets and cities.

- Designing out crime focuses on the development of products and technology that make it significantly harder for a criminal to carry out their intended attack.

- Even large organisations can make operational mistakes, as was seen in the Project Champion review.

CHECK YOUR KNOWLEDGE

1. Who is responsible for crime prevention and why?

2. Provide ten recommendations that align with Cornish and Clarke's 25 techniques of crime prevention.

3. List the six categories that fall under the CRAVED mnemonic.

4. Explain the four elements of the 'hot model' and consider what makes them 'hot'.

5. How would you explain the term 'situational crime prevention' to a police cadet (under 18s)?

6. Make a range of practical suggestions linked to CPTED that would better protect your local housing estate, town centre or retail park.

7. Why did Project Champion fail and why is it an example of ethical and legitimacy shortcomings on the part of the police?

Sample answers are provided at the end of this book.

FURTHER READING

ARTICLES, BOOKS AND CHAPTERS

Beauregard, E and Martineau, M (2015) An Application of CRAVED to the Choice of Victim in Sexual Homicide: A Routine Activity Approach. *Crime Science*, 4(24): 1–11.
This article applies the CRAVED mnemonic to other crime types such as sexual homicide and will enhance your topic understanding.

Design Council (2011) *Designing Out Crime: A Designers' Guide*. [online] Available at: www.designcouncil.org.uk/fileadmin/uploads/dc/Documents/designersGuide_digital_0_0.pdf (accessed 6 May 2023).

A comprehensive guide looking at the relationship between crime from a design perspective and the creative solutions to tackle different types of criminality.

Patel, C (2018) The 'Ideal' Victim of International Criminal Law. *The European Journal of International Law*, 29(3): 703–24.
Read pages 709–13 to further explore Christie's work on the ideal victim.

Statewatch.org (2010) Project Champion Review. [online] Available at: www.statewatch.org/media/documents/news/2010/oct/uk-project-champion-police-report.pdf (accessed 6 May 2023).
Review of the failings of the proposed West Midlands Police Counter Terrorism initiative 'Project Champion' by Sara Thornton, then Chief Constable of Thames Valley Police.

WEBSITES

Hern, A (2018) Fitness Tracking App Strava Gives Away Location of Secret US Army Bases. *The Guardian*, 28 January. [online]. Available at: www.theguardian.com/world/2018/jan/28/fitness-tracking-app-gives-away-location-of-secret-us-army-bases (accessed 6 May 2023).
An interesting article that discusses how an activity-tracking application has the scope to reveal sensitive information about a US army base with the potential for extreme consequences.

Hollie Guard (2022) Safeguarding People Where It Matters. [online] Available at: https://hollieguard.com (accessed 6 May 2023).
A mobile phone application that pinpoints your location and immediately notifies your contacts if you feel that you are in danger.

CHAPTER 6
PARTNERSHIP WORKING IN CRIME PREVENTION

LEARNING OBJECTIVES

AFTER READING THIS CHAPTER YOU WILL BE ABLE TO:

- understand what INTERPOL and EUROPOL are;
- understand the impact of political decisions like Brexit on international policing;
- understand the core principles of multi-agency working within England and Wales;
- critically consider the strengths and weaknesses of current partnership practice.

INTRODUCTION

One of the most important areas you will need to examine as an officer is partnership working, which is multi-agency working with other organisations who also have responsibilities for safeguarding the public, including probation and social services. These national frameworks often include statutory (legal requirements by government legislation) responsibilities; however, sometimes the police will work with other agencies voluntarily. One of the guiding principles of partnership working is Policing Priorities. These are decided at a local level and involve the police and other professionals consulting with the public to decide what to prioritise in a specific service area (College of Policing, 2023c).

However, police involvement is not limited to England and Wales; the police have also had a role with international crime prevention, in both European Union Agency for Law Enforcement Cooperation (EUROPOL) (policing within the European Union) and the International Criminal Police Organization (INTERPOL) (international policing, across the world) (EUROPOL, 2022a; INTERPOL, 2023c). These organisations are supranational (beyond the control of any one nation) and are aimed at preventing very serious offences and organised crime. The chapter begins with an introduction to INTERPOL before considering practice at an increasingly localised level, moving on to EUROPOL before examining multi-agency working in England and Wales.

INTRODUCING INTERPOL

INTERPOL has 195 member countries; it polices in each of these and facilitates data sharing on crime and offenders and provides both operational and technical support. Its current priorities are organised crime, cybercrime and terrorism, offences which often cross national borders. INTERPOL links even member states which do not have diplomatic relations or specific treaties with one another. It does not take a stance on political issues and stays within the legal boundaries of member states (INTERPOL, 2023c).

The General Secretariat is the co-ordinator for daily operations and is run by the Secretary General, staffed by civilians as well as police officers, and is based in Lyon with offices in a number of other nations as well. In every country, the National Central Bureau (NCB) is the main contact for both the General Secretariat and other NCBs. It is run by national police and is almost always directed by (at a national level) the government branch which controls policing; in England and Wales this is the Home Office. INTERPOL is governed by a General Assembly, made up of all member countries, which meets annually in a decision-making capacity (INTERPOL, 2023c).

EVIDENCE-BASED POLICING

ADVANCED INFORMATION SHARING

INTERPOL uses I-24/7 to allow service and database access in each member state, keeping member countries in constant communication with each other and the General Secretariat via a secure network. Police networks also contribute to this, and these include experts in specific areas, such as human trafficking, who conduct conferences and working groups to share and devise best practice for international offences. Expertise is also provided by the General Secretariat on data analysis, locating absconding offenders and fugitives, and forensics. Police databases, including details of offences and offenders from all member countries, are included on centrally managed databases which all members can access.

INTERPOL also provides training to ensure local police can work effectively with INTERPOL, including training, networking and assistance with operations. It also provides research into emerging patterns and types of crime and innovative ways to prevent this. One of its better-known functions is to issue 'red notices' which alert police forces in member countries to the fact that there is a dangerous fugitive at large. INTERPOL is useful in communicating to government what the police need (INTERPOL, 2023c). Consider the ethical issues associated with international policing: do any potential negatives outweigh the positives?

UNITED KINGDOM MEMBERSHIP OF INTERPOL AND THE ROLE OF THE NATIONAL CRIME AGENCY

Although the UK has different jurisdictions for the nations within it, its membership of INTERPOL is as a whole country. Organised crime is considered a significant problem and a national security priority in the UK, along with terrorism (INTERPOL, 2023b).

The NCB of the UK is located in Manchester rather than London, and is also part of the National Crime Agency (NCA), which focuses on organised crime and international offending and risks to security. Its main priorities are cybercrime and fraud, serious and organised crime, the strengthening of UK borders, and the protection of vulnerable people, including children and young adults. INTERPOL Manchester acts as the UK co-ordinator for international crime and provides intelligence and specialist support to operations through the use of INTERPOL networks and facilitating communication between UK police services and international agencies on a global scale (INTERPOL, 2023b).

Manchester also helps to protect 14 Overseas Territories belonging to the UK; to assist with this, it has Sub-Bureaus responsible to it in Anguilla, Bermuda, Gibraltar, the Cayman Islands, Monserrat, the British Virgin Islands, Turks and Caicos. Each of these Sub-Bureaus has delegated to it a designated legal authority, responsible for the region. These are answerable to the NCB in Manchester (INTERPOL, 2023b).

The NCB also communicates relevant patterns in international offending to local police services and helps them to monitor the trafficking of both products and people. The NCB prioritises offences against vulnerable people (especially children), human trafficking, hunting for fugitives who have/may have committed serious crimes and financial offending. INTERPOL works with all relevant local police services, as well as the Ministry of Defence Police, British Transport Police and the Civil Nuclear Constabulary as all have a role in the prevention of international offending and/or may have intelligence on fugitives and the capacity to track them down (INTERPOL, 2023b).

CONTROVERSY SURROUNDING INTERPOL'S POLICY ON POLITICS

INTERPOL's policy of neutrality has caused issues; it has been accused of a lack of transparency and of unquestioningly issuing 'red notices' on behalf of member states. This includes those which are run by dictators or could be described as 'oppressive', often either run by dictatorships or with limited democracy, suppressing opposition; this has included finding and arresting opponents of Vladimir Putin on charges these individuals refute and allege are politically motivated (Jacobs, 2021). INTERPOL has also criticised the UK government for policies relating to terrorism which it deemed too extreme, accusations the Home Secretary (in charge of policing) at the time, Jacqui Smith, strongly refuted (Oliver and Agencies, 2007).

REFLECTIVE PRACTICE 6.1

PERSONAL REFLECTIONS OF INTERPOL'S POLICIES

Reflect upon your views regarding international policing and the ethical and practical implications of INTERPOL's policy of neutrality and chosen priorities.

Consider your own beliefs about national powers and how far you think national sovereignty should take precedence (a country's ability to decide its own laws and policies as more important than co-operation between nations). List different types of crime you are aware of and identify the level to which they impact members of the public both in the UK and globally.

Reflect upon your views on how far a government should go to determine its treatment of citizens and how far the international community should intervene.

- How do you feel about the concept of an international police force?

- Does this worry you or do you find it reassuring? Explain your answer.

- Do you agree with INTERPOL's list of priorities?

- Who else may be involved in assisting victims and apprehending offenders, outside of law enforcement?

- Can these organisations work internationally?

- Do you think INTERPOL was justified in criticising British policy?

- Would your opinion change if it was a completely different policy?

- Do they have a duty to follow up all arrest warrants, even those from oppressive regimes?

- What are the pros and cons of doing so?

- What issues may arise if they treat some nations differently?

- What do you think is the reason for INTERPOL maintaining a neutral stance on the politics of member states?

- Do you think this should change?

- If INTERPOL refused to follow warrants issued for allegedly political reasons, what might the impact be?

Hints: Research any non-governmental organisations (NGOs) which work with vulnerable people; consider if any UK-based charities have an international focus – INTERPOL is not the only international organisation which the UK co-operates with – it also works with EUROPOL.

Sample answers are provided at the end of this book.

INTRODUCING EUROPOL

EUROPOL is comprised of member states within the European Union (EU); it supports operations within these states but does not initiate these (EUROPOL, 2022a). EUROPOL works with other nations too and prioritises human trafficking, cybercrime, drugs, illegal immigration, counterfeiting of euros, money laundering, gangs, VAT fraud, terrorism, organised crime, asset tracing, intellectual property offences and the smuggling of cigarettes (EUROPOL, 2022a, 2022b).

EUROPOL produces reports on patterns of crime in the EU, with a particular focus on terrorism. It has specialist services, including information linking, searching and storing, and member states can make use of these. It is accountable to the EU Council of Ministers for Justice and Home Affairs. The Council controls and guides EUROPOL, appointing Executive Directors and their Deputies, controlling the budget in partnership with the EU Parliament which also has joint control over regulating EUROPOL. It is the Council which compiles the report on its work and presents this to the EU Parliament (EUROPOL, 2022a). Figure 6.1 is a graphic which lays out the command structure of EUROPOL.

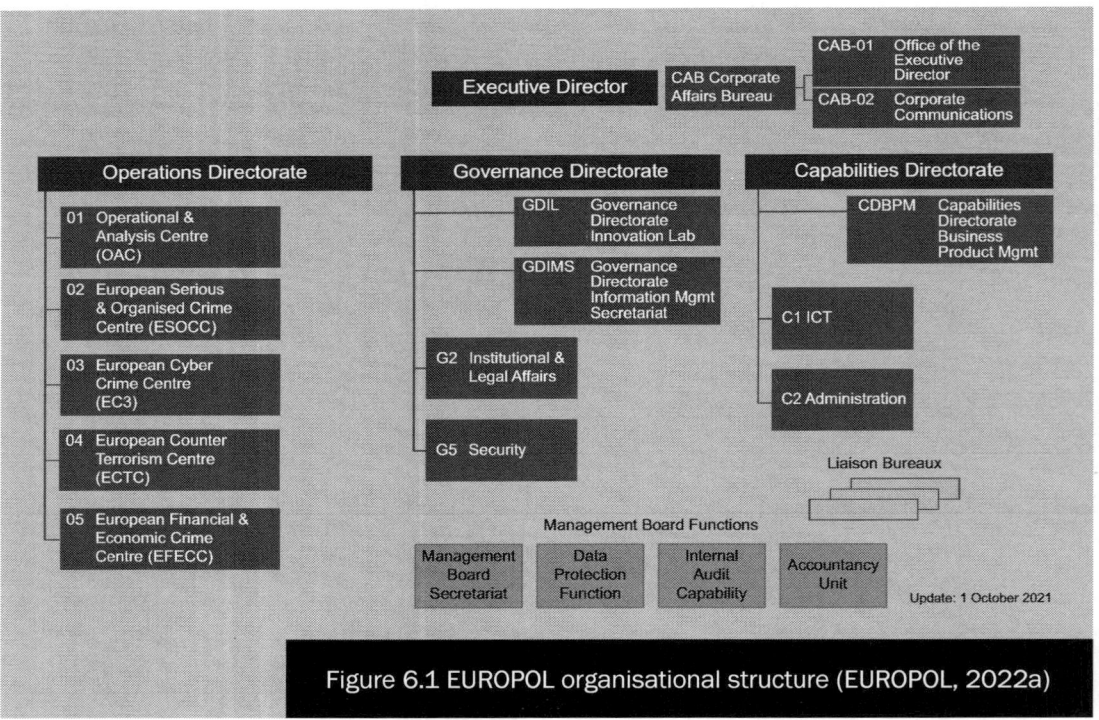

Figure 6.1 EUROPOL organisational structure (EUROPOL, 2022a)

The current guidelines, known as the EUROPOL Regulation, facilitate a strong role for EUROPOL in tackling cybercrime, serious and organised crime and terrorism, as well as facilitating close co-operation among law enforcement authorities within the EU (EUROPOL, 2022a, 2022b).

IMPACT OF BREXIT

Prior to Brexit, the UK was part of the arrangements outlined above (EUROPOL, 2021). However, as it is no longer a member of the EU, new negotiations on partnership working were needed and in 2021 these concluded. The UK now has a working relationship with EUROPOL (EUROPOL, 2021, 2022b). This Working and Administrative Arrangement is part of the EU–UK Trade and Cooperative Agreement (TCA) and has clarified the law enforcement elements of this. The arrangements include providing liaison officers to facilitate work between EUROPOL and the NCA (including NCA officers based in the headquarters of EUROPOL), and access to EUROPOL's secure system for messaging, as well as a presence at operational meetings with EUROPOL and the authority to call such meetings and to make contributions to them (EUROPOL, 2021; NCA, 2021). The UK can also still contribute to projects which include analysis and can make use of the analytical capabilities of EUROPOL, co-ordination of these and efficient data exchanges. These arrangements may provide reassurance in terms of daily practices, honour-based violence and serious and organised crime; however, there are some possible downsides to the current arrangements.

CRITICAL THINKING ACTIVITY 6.1

LEVELS 5 AND 6

Consider how much international co-operation is needed to ensure public protection.

- Examine the list of EUROPOL's priorities and briefly consider what harm is being prevented by tackling each of these.

- Take two examples and devise a 'for and against' table regarding their inclusion in the list of EUROPOL's top priorities.

- How do you think these compare with British national security interests?

- Do you think Brexit has had a positive or negative impact on the UK in terms of national security and international crime? Explain your answer.

- Outline any counterarguments to your ideas.

Hint: EUROPOL is answerable only to European politicians, and the fact the UK will no longer have a role in steering the work of this international agency could be seen as a problem as it may mean UK security priorities are ignored and protection of British interests is not considered a priority in terms of resource allocation. However, it could also be argued that the flexibility offered in a Working Arrangement allows the UK to determine what is right for it and to co-operate as much or as little as desired, by abiding by current agreements or seeking to renegotiate them, if the government feels the need.

Sample answers are provided at the end of this book.

POLICING SPOTLIGHT

INTRODUCING THE CROWN PROSECUTION SERVICE

It is also important to consider the role of the Crown Prosecution Service (CPS), which is the organisation that determines whether a public prosecution will be carried out in England and Wales. The CPS operates by seeing if a case passes two tests: likelihood of successful prosecution and if a case is in the public interest. The police need to provide the CPS with sufficient information to determine the answers to these (CPS, 2022b). These tests are both controversial as it may be subjective what is and is not in the public interest and may mean that the law is not applied equally to all citizens. Furthermore, the CPS effectively has to guess at what a jury may find persuasive; this cannot be deemed to be 100 per cent accurate as a test, and officers and victims may be left frustrated by refusal to take a case forward and a victim may even feel disbelieved. For further information on the role of the CPS, please see the book entitled *Police Procedure and Evidence in the Criminal Justice System* (Archer and Ellison, 2023).

REFLECTIVE PRACTICE 6.1

LEVEL 6

THE CPS AND YOUR PERSONAL PERSPECTIVE

Imagine if you were head of a victims' rights campaign group and one of your clients is a victim of historic child abuse.

- Consider any concerns you may have about the CPS tests.

Next, imagine you are a youth worker attempting to help deprived young people succeed and keep them out of the criminal justice system.

- Consider what your perspective on these tests may be.

Hints: Victims may feel disbelieved if the CPS does not prosecute their case; they may feel that failure to meet the criteria needed for a probable conviction may mean that the CPS do not believe them. They may also feel denied any chance to obtain justice. Young people can find themselves in the criminal justice system and their job prospects and life chances ruined by a criminal conviction. If the offence is indictable but not severe and/or the victim is willing to accept an Out of Court Disposal, the CPS may decide a prosecution is not in the public interest (only indictable offences require CPS approval) (CPS, 2022a).

Sample answers are provided at the end of this book.

PUBLIC PROTECTION AND SAFEGUARDING OF VULNERABLE PEOPLE

Multi-agency working involves co-operation with other organisations responsible for public protection such as probation and the prison service. These are described as Multi-Agency Public Protection Arrangements (MAPPA) regarding serious and violent offenders and protecting the public from these; they consider sexual and domestic abusers and other violent criminals. They monitor them and share intelligence and data with other relevant agencies, including risk assessments (College of Policing, 2023c) and information sharing agreements. Information may be shared with civil courts and other organisations with which there may be Service Level Agreements, which include taking joint action beyond simply sharing data. This may involve a Multi-Agency Risk Assessment Conference (MARAC). Local crime and justice partnerships ensure that local priorities are the focus of all responsible agencies (College of Policing, 2023c). Policing Priorities may be set with the police and crime commissioner, with the co-operation and support of police.

Community safety partnerships focus on the local population, particularly vulnerable people, and include the police as well as local authorities, fire and rescue, healthcare professionals and probation. These have statutory (legally required) obligations to protect the public. Safeguarding adults and children's boards also consider people with specific vulnerabilities who may be victimised owing to these or encounter specific types of crime such as child, elder or domestic abuse (College of Policing, 2023c). Specialist domestic violence courts may also liaise with the police and officers may find Independent Domestic/Sexual Violence Advocates (IDVAs and ISVAs, respectively) to be useful in terms of supporting and communicating with victims (College of Policing, 2023c). These are frameworks that are examined in greater detail later in this chapter but first you must consider who else officers may need to work with. For further information, please see the book entitled *Policing Mental Health, Vulnerability and Risk* (Williams, 2023).

WORKING WITH THE THIRD SECTOR

In addition to their work with ISVAs and IDVAs, police may also work with third sector organisations. These may reach victims and wider communities in a way the police cannot.

POLICING SPOTLIGHT

WORKING WITH WOMEN'S AID

In addition to working with victims signposted to them by the police, Women's Aid (a charity which supports women who have been victims of violence and abuse) also provides training to officers in order to strengthen understanding of victims and responses to domestic violence and abuse (WMP, nd; Women's Aid, 2022). This is an example of non-statutory working, not enforced or even guided by legislation but rather a collaborative response to a need within the community.

CRITICAL THINKING ACTIVITY 6.2

LEVEL 4

ADVANTAGES OF INFORMAL PARTNERSHIPS

- Why do you think the police may need support in tackling domestic violence and abuse?

- What advantages do third sector organisations like Women's Aid have over the police regarding communicating effectively with victims?

Hint: The police have traditionally been perceived as dealing with domestic violence and abuse badly; not taking it seriously enough, not understanding how victims are impacted and showing frustration if they did not feel able to continue to co-operate; however, organisations like Women's Aid have long called for changes to this (Women's Aid, 2022). Consider how this may impact a victim's decision regarding who to talk to.

Sample answers are provided at the end of this book.

INFORMAL PARTNERSHIPS: SCHOOLS, MENTAL HEALTH SERVICES AND THE WIDER COMMUNITY

The police also work in a less structured way with organsiations such as schools, where they work collaboratively to improve both student safety and behaviour, though this is not uncontroversial (owing to fears that children may be intimidated, and responses may be disproportionate). Some such arrangements have been regarded by those involved as a success (Birmingham Police and Schools Panel, nd).

After years of reputational damage concerning the treatment of mentally ill people, the police are now regarded as more compassionate (although areas of bad practice still exist). However, this has led to fears that other organisations may be overly reliant upon them and use the police to simply stall for time, owing to their greater powers to detain compared to such agencies such as NHS Community Mental Health Teams (HMICFRS, 2018).

REFLECTIVE PRACTICE 6.2

LEVELS 4-6

Examine the role officers play in the partnerships outlined above and consider who they are intending to support. Then revisit the list of organisations and individuals the police must work with and evaluate their involvement in public protection and partnerships involved in this.

- Do you believe that it is appropriate for the police to be tackling such issues as children's safety within schools and mental health issues in the community above?

- What factors have you considered when determining your position on this?

- Why do you think statutory agencies have been selected to have legal obligations to protect the public?

- Do you think any other agencies should have this legal responsibility? (Keep a note of these initial impressions to examine if these agencies are considered when you examine MAPPA frameworks and informal arrangements in more detail.)

- If you feel more agencies should be included, which and why?

- If you feel the list is complete, why are the organisations already listed sufficient?

Sample answers are provided at the end of this book.

POLICING SPOTLIGHT

BRITISH TRANSPORT POLICE: 'TOGETHER WE CAN STOP SEXUAL HARASSMENT'

The police can also work with the wider community through public education. For example, the British Transport Police's (2023) 'Together We Can Stop Sexual Harassment' campaign engaged directly with the public, with the aim of directly involving them in reducing such offending, encouraging them to either challenge non-violent harassment, ensure they remained physically close to the scene in the hope that this would deter the harasser, or actively contact the British Transport Police, thus drawing them into collaboration (British Transport Police, 2023).

Consider if there are any possible dangers with such a campaign and what the unintended consequences could be. You should conduct a cost–benefit analysis to explore if this is a positive contribution to public protection overall. Ensure that you evaluate whether this reduces police accountability for the prevention of such offences.

RELEVANT LEGISLATION AND STATUTORY MEASURES TO ENSURE ACCOUNTABILITY

The statutory duty to reduce both offending and disorder stems from the Crime and Disorder Act 1998, which mandates partnership approaches to community safety, resulting in community safety partnerships. The Criminal Justice Act 2003 stipulates that MAPPA working and information sharing regarding risk assessments is mandatory. However, the work of these partnerships must be evaluated to ensure it is fit for purpose.

Audits are meant to hold services accountable (evaluate whether they do a good job or not and ensure something is done if they are failing). Audits consider services provided by the relevant agencies and consider anything that may stop a service user from receiving strong provision from each one and the multi-agency partnership as a whole. Agencies are responsible for setting the terms of reference (remit) for the audit as well as consultations (with service users, the community and professionals) and agreeing how to carry out the audit (College of Policing, 2023c).

When working in relation to domestic violence and abuse, all partners must take part in audits and data collection must ensure accuracy and take a holistic approach so that the true scale of the issue is understood. Reporting, effectiveness of current policies, any signs of offending and level of provision all have to be monitored and any gaps identified. Police Chiefs are responsible for ensuring this process can be carried out and accurate data collected; in addition to the elements highlighted above, this must also facilitate a strategic assessment by the police service and provide responses to what the data reveals (College of Policing, 2023c).

Even with this level of care, it is impossible to ensure accurate data due to factors such as insufficient data from agencies which focus on other areas; voluntary (third sector) organisations that do not automatically share information with the police; inaccuracy of public surveys and the 'dark figure of crime', which means that (owing to underreporting and under-recording) we cannot know how much domestic violence and abuse there is; inadequacy of traditional policing methods as this crime is hidden; and the lack of a specific offence type that allows for specific recording of domestic violence and abuse. However, soliciting the help of a third sector organisation that victims may feel more comfortable speaking to can improve the quality of such data. Furthermore, anonymity is paramount in public consultations, especially with regard to service users (College of Policing, 2023c).

Despite being set out in the Domestic Violence, Crime and Victims Act 2004, domestic homicide reviews (DHRs) only became mandatory in 2011. These are set in motion by the chair of the community safety partnership within a month of a referral by a relevant agency, including the police. The aim of these is to learn from mistakes as opposed to identifying which professionals are culpable for them. DHRs conduct multi-agency reviews at a local level and examine the death of an individual who is 16 or over and seems to have died through violence, neglect or abuse at the hands of someone who lived with the victim, a relative, or an intimate partner or former partner (College of Policing, 2023c). The police have a statutory duty to involve themselves, along with other services including NHS Trusts and probation services; others may be instructed to participate, including the CPS. The police must also be represented on the review panel and if the police are investigating or there is a prosecution the senior investigating officer needs to be consulted on the terms of reference so that the two investigations do not conflict for the review; however, the chair must be independent (College of Policing, 2023c).

Domestic violence/abuse forums are often used to:

- establish needed services for victims and their children (legally also victims);
- consult with victims;
- improve networking among and co-ordination of local services as well as any relevant training for these;
- developing strategies for delivery;
- educating the public;
- improve service delivery;
- review cases;
- organise prevention programmes;
- provide education regarding domestic violence and abuse for schools.

It is important for forums to establish clear aims and strategies so that these can be scrutinised regarding their success levels. Forums should not be held at police stations and officers should try to avoid setting agendas or chairing meetings; the chairperson often is rotated in order to give sufficient prominence to third sector experts (College of Policing, 2023c). All relevant agencies must have specific domestic violence and abuse policies which can be evaluated and co-ordinated by the forum. Where possible, specialist officers should be involved and a domestic violence and abuse unit established. The forum needs to consider a MARAC policy, a resources pack for professionals, a statement regarding policy, systems for scrutinising and assessing the work of the forum as part of a wider policing strategy, information sharing agreements, information for victims and training for professionals (College of Policing, 2023c). Forums are measured by any improvement in the following areas:

- provision;
- policy;
- service use;
- safety;
- satisfaction of service users;
- delivery;
- practice;
- consultation;
- development of strategies.

LEGISLATION AND ACCOUNTABILITY MEASURES FOCUSED ON SPECIFIC OFFENCES AND DEMOGRAPHICS

Local safeguarding children boards (LSCBs) also require careful co-ordination and the local authority of each area is responsible for this. LSCBs are a statutory (legal) requirement and form the basis of agreements on co-operation to improve child welfare (College of Policing, 2023c). This responsibility is enshrined in the Children Act 2004.

There is also a role for non-statutory agencies in protecting vulnerable people; third sector organisations may choose to be members and domestic violence forums must be represented as these frameworks help to evaluate and propose services to families and so those with expertise are extremely helpful to this process (College of Policing, 2023c). Safeguarding adults boards (SABs) perform a similar function to LSCBs for adults. These were made compulsory under the Care Act 2014. They apply to vulnerable adults, defined as those who need support and care, regardless of who provides this; as a result of their needs, they cannot defend themselves from neglect or abuse or are subject to these (College of Policing, 2023c).

The SAB must lead adult safeguarding, establish frameworks and ensure all agencies do their utmost to prevent such abuse and neglect; it is a statutory requirement that the police are represented, and chairpersons are chosen for skill or expertise, not because they belong to a specific organisation. Should serious mistakes be made, such as a death of a vulnerable adult as a result of abuse or neglect or a living person has been subjected to severe levels of abuse or neglect, a Safeguarding Adult Review (SAR) must be conducted, and it may be appropriate to begin reviews into similar cases. The police have a statutory duty to co-operate with these and specific lessons to be learned must be highlighted and applied to casework in the future; these findings must also comprise part of the annual report and relevant plans or action points must also be referenced (College of Policing, 2023c).

The range of agencies involved is designed to promote best practice. However, should a case result in tragedy, these same organisations will be tasked with exposing wrongdoing owing to the complexity of these frameworks. It may also be difficult to hold specific agencies to account as the responsibility is effectively pooled. However, statutory obligations ensure that not only do specific professionals have a legal duty to follow policy but that it is those who most need to learn from tragedies and who ostensibly have the requisite expertise who investigate such cases.

THE ROLE OF POLICE AND CRIME COMMISSIONERS

Police and crime commissioners (PCCs) must work with their local community safety partnerships but they are not the responsible authority (legally responsible and in charge), the Police Reform and Social Responsibility Act 2011 provides a protocol for how such collaboration should manifest but there is flexibility in this to allow local concerns to be prioritised. One element that is stipulated is that the PCC and community safety partnerships must consider each other's priorities when forming respective plans and proposals (College of Policing, 2023c).

CO-OPERATING WITH MEMBERS OF THE COMMUNITY WHO ASSIST POLICE ACCOUNTABILITY

In addition to the police co-operating with DHRs and other MAPPA frameworks, PCCs may also establish community-based scrutiny panels. These examine cases (usually selected at random) of police interaction with the public to check that both statutory and policy-based requirements have been met (SYP, 2022; WMP, 2023a). They are comprised of members of the local community, who may be youth workers, magistrates, academics and community leaders; anyone can volunteer to be part of such a board (SYP, 2022).

Panel members generally view bodycam footage to decide upon the appropriateness of the response of the officers in question. However, in some cases notes may be all that are provided. Stop and search powers and use of force are common focuses for scrutiny panels, but other areas may also be considered by a dedicated panel (SYP, 2022). The aim is to improve both police accountability and communication with the public; it affords officers the opportunity to both explain decisions and examine public reactions to them (SYP, 2022; WMP, 2023a). However, scrutiny panels are not comprised of experts and lack any statutory authority. They can only make recommendations which will then be fed back to relevant officers; thus, their findings may not even be known in the police service as a whole. The PCC and senior officers do not have to act upon any recommendations but should report any suggestions to the relevant officers and their commanding officers and share findings at annual conferences (WMP, 2023a).

CRITICAL THINKING ACTIVITY 6.3

LEVELS 4, 5 AND 6

EVALUATING ACCOUNTABILITY FRAMEWORKS

Consider how the processes and partnerships above should hold the police accountable and examine the description of how partnerships should promote accountability. Ensure you refer to the description of the role taken by the PCC and explanation of the function of scrutiny panels and who can sit on them.

- What are the advantages of current partnership structures?

- What negatives can you identify regarding current mechanisms for accountability?

- Do you think the PCC has an appropriate level of responsibility? Why or why not?

- On a scale of one to ten, how effective do you believe scrutiny panels to be? Provide some examples.

- If they were dissolved, what would be the impact on police accountability?

- Do you think they should be given statutory authority to impose their recommendations?

- Consider any counterarguments to your decision.

Hint: Remember that many of the same organisations responsible for making any mistakes are also key in the accountability process. Also keep in mind that these are the experts in this area and know the policies and procedures that should have been followed. Remember that the PCC is a locally elected politician, not a police officer.

Sample answers are provided at the end of this book.

SUMMARY OF KEY CONCEPTS

This chapter has explored some of the following key concepts.

- INTERPOL: an international law enforcement body, spanning over several continents.

- EUROPOL: an international law enforcement body which focuses on threats to and within the EU.

- Accountability measures: mechanisms that ensure that the police are using their powers appropriately and tackling issues in public protection effectively.

- Multi-agency working: collaboration between many organisations to promote public protection.

- Statutory requirements: legally enforceable obligations, outlined in legislation.

CHECK YOUR KNOWLEDGE

1. What is the purpose of INTERPOL?

2. What is the UK's relationship with EUROPOL?

3. How does the CPS decide if a case is going to be prosecuted or not?

4. What statutory partnerships would be involved with helping a victim of domestic violence and abuse?

5. Who else might you wish to informally partner with in order to provide the victim with optimum resources?

6. Who else must you consider when thinking about provision in this case? What statutory organisations could support anyone else impacted?

7. Should something tragic occur, what scrutiny processes might you be subject to?

Sample answers are provided at the end of this book.

FURTHER READING

These resources will help you to enhance your understanding of the subjects covered in the chapter.

WEBSITES

College of Policing (2023) Partnership Working and Multi-Agency Responses/Mechanisms. [online] Available at: www.college.police.uk/app/major-investigation-and-public-protection/domestic-abuse/partnership-working-and-multi-agency-responsesmechanisms (accessed 8 March 2023).

Crown Prosecution Service (CPS) (2022b) The Principles We Follow. [online] Available at: www.cps.gov.uk/principles-we-follow (accessed 8 March 2023).

INTERPOL (2023c) United Kingdom. [online] Available at: www.INTERPOL.int/en/Who-we-are/Member-countries/Europe/UNITED-KINGDOM (accessed 8 March 2023).

National Crime Agency (2021) NCA and EUROPOL Sign Up to a New Working Arrangement. [online] Available at: https://nationalcrimeagency.gov.uk/news/nca-and-europol-sign-up-to-a-new-working-arrangement (accessed 8 March 2023).

ARTICLES, BOOKS AND CHAPTERS

EUROPOL (2021) *Working and Administrative Arrangements Establishing Cooperative Relations between the Competent Authorities of the United Kingdom of Great Britain and Northern Ireland and the European Union Agency for Law Enforcement Cooperation.* [online] Available at: www.EUROPOL.europa.eu/cms/sites/default/files/documents/wa_with_united_kingdom_-_implementing_the_tca.pdf (accessed 8 March 2023).

SAMPLE ANSWERS

CHAPTER 1

CRITICAL THINKING ACTIVITY 1.1

Level 4 and 5 answers may include:

- Citizens less able or willing to report crimes.

- Citizens less able or willing to share information with the police.

- Reduced perceptions of 'reassurance policing' and the availability of officers to respond to local crime problems.

- Police forces are less aware of local crime and disorder issues in the area and therefore the lack of response could undermine public confidence.

Level 6 answers may include:

Where citizens have lower perceptions of police legitimacy, they may be less inclined to obey the authority of the police and less inclined to obey the law. This could lead to more hostile encounters between the police and citizens, making it more difficult for you to secure willing co-operation. This may result in increased use of handcuffs and use of force, which can also contribute towards lower perceptions of legitimacy in themselves. Lower perceptions of police legitimacy could also lead to citizens committing more crime and being less reluctant to report crimes they have been victim to themselves.

CRITICAL THINKING ACTIVITY 1.2

Answers may include:

- PCSOs are seen as there to 'support' the community and not for a crime control purpose.

- No formal powers of enforcement so citizens may be more willing to share information if they do not believe they will be arrested.

- Based in the neighbourhood for a longer period than a police constable so may be perceived as more trustworthy.

- May be perceived to have a better understanding of the local area and residents, and therefore potentially be more effective at responding to crime issues.

- May be seen to engage in activities beyond what is often achievable by an immediate 999 response (more likely to engage in longer-term measures).

CRITICAL THINKING ACTIVITY 1.3

Level 4 and 5 answers may include:

- They provide a visual deterrent.

- They provide an opportunity for residents and the police to discuss issues of concern relating to crime and disorder, which can increase public confidence for citizens and provide an additional source of information for officers.

- It can strengthen collective efficacy as the volunteers demonstrate active citizenship and this could also encourage other residents to keep an eye out for potential threats or risks in their area

Level 6 answers may include:

- Provide advice on how to protect homes and belongings, for example, ensuring windows and doors are locked, installing window sashes and locks, immobilisers on cars etc.

- Provide branded livery (or advice on how to obtain this from established schemes such as the Neighbourhood Watch scheme) for residents to display in their windows or on lampposts in the area.

- Propose creating a neighbourhood WhatsApp group where they can share updates with each other.

- Encourage citizens to take part in existing community safeguarding initiatives such as street patrols etc.

CRITICAL THINKING ACTIVITY 1.4

Level 4, 5 and 6 answers may include:

- An open-ended question asking which crime issue is the most important.

SAMPLE ANSWERS   135

- Provide a list of options of local crime issues and ask them to rank them in order of importance.

- Ask their views on local crime issues or hot spots you may be aware of.

- Ask them to pinpoint certain problem locations on a map.

- Ask if they are satisfied with the current police resources deployed to a certain area.

- Ask if they believe more policing resources should be allocated to certain areas.

Level 6 answers may include:

1. May not end up with a consensus: not all options may be viable or realistic from a policing process perspective or may be time-consuming.

2. Cost-effective, quick, may encourage youths to participate; however, may not be accessible to all.

3. They may have a better idea of wider problems in the community and how this particular issue fits into those wider issues; may not be seen as democratic by wider community members; may be time-consuming.

CRITICAL THINKING ACTIVITY 1.6

1. You could seek to hold an additional community meeting and put forward all these issues for community members to report on; you could distribute a survey or create a social media poll.

2. and 3. Answers may include the following:

- You could ask the school to stage an intervention with their pupils as most of the incidents involve one school; you could see if the bus station has CCTV from which students could be identified; you could ask the bus station if they have security present or you could ask PCSOs to patrol the bus station after school hours.

- In relation to the thefts, you could ask the shopkeepers to install CCTV and also probe as to what other security functions they have to minimise opportunities for offending (security tags on alcohol bottles or putting these behind the counter, for example).

- You could ask the local authority to support with the littering. Ask citizens to raise this directly with the local authority too.

- You could ask the school to have some staff/security members stand outside the café on the road for an hour after school begins and encourage students to go into school. You could ask the school to remind students about late attendance and perhaps enforce a stricter policy, even on a temporary basis. You could ask a PCSO to conduct foot patrols there, perhaps on a more occasional basis.

4. Disorder at the bus stop could be quantified, as could thefts at the shop. Citizen perceptions should be monitored on an ongoing basis in relation to the other issues to understand how successful these measures are and whether additional measures may be required.

CHECK YOUR KNOWLEDGE

1. The neighbourhood policing model was introduced in response to citizen concerns that crime (and therefore fear of crime) was rising, which led to corresponding decreases in public confidence. Neighbourhood policing was designed to have dedicated policing teams within neighbourhoods who would not only reassure citizens that the police were addressing crime, but would proactively help address crimes.

2. Engaging communities, problem solving and targeting activity.

3. Answers may include setting up community meetings, engaging with citizens while on patrol, community mapping and building networks with existing organisations, using social media to connect with organisations and meeting with community leaders.

4. Scanning, Analysis, Response and Assessment.

5. PCSOs provide a vital visible deterrent and reassurance function (within a wider trust and intelligence-building function) which can help build community trust in times of austerity where police constables may have less time to engage in such activities.

6. Hot spots can allow neighbourhood officers to target their resources towards a micro-location, which increases its prospect of crime reduction and deterrence. It can, for example, direct where PCSO patrols would be most effectively served.

CHAPTER 2

CRITICAL THINKING ACTIVITY 2.1

Level 4 answers may include:

- 999 call logs.

- Reported crime data.

- Data from the NHS indicating where violent offences have occurred.

- Data from schools on pupil truancy and reports of issues within the school.

- Data from the local authority on increased civil disorder such as graffiti or criminal damage in public spaces.

Level 5 and 6 answers may include:

- Not all reported crimes may be recorded accurately; for example, if a crime occurs in a public location but is reported at a home, the home address may be recorded.

- Where public locations are over a bigger area, such as a large park, this may lead to most crimes being recorded at one location when they were more spread out.

- Errors in reporting or spelling may lead to some locations not being picked up.

CRITICAL THINKING ACTIVITY 2.2

Level 4 answers may include:

- Increased resource demands and fewer officers may mean there are fewer officers available to conduct foot patrols as officers are busy responding to 999 calls. Where officers are available, they may not be able to remain within that location for a sufficiently long period of time. Different officers may also need to attend each time, which can be problematic if an additional aim of the patrol was building trust with the community, a tactic often used by neighbourhood officers as seen in Chapter 1.

Level 5 and 6 answers may include:

- The longer-term implications of hot spot policing methods as a method of crime reduction are still unclear; however, as hot spot policing methods do not attempt to address the underlying root causes of crime, they are unlikely to solve crime within these areas. The limited evidence examining the lasting effects of hot spot policing found that after 90 days crime reduction effects had disappeared, which indicates this is not a long-term strategy.

REFLECTIVE PRACTICE 2.1

- Explain the evidence base for hot spot policing and foot patrols to your colleague.

- Brainstorm other ideas which may be more effective and which your partner does support, which you can propose to your sergeant once your patrol is complete.

- Explain to your partner that educating citizens in keeping their possessions safe can make the target less suitable as it becomes more difficult to steal and therefore less attractive as a target.

CRITICAL THINKING ACTIVITY 2.3

- Advising nightclubs to increase CCTV may make it easier to identify who has been dealing by (scanning and) sharing video evidence with the police; this can make it quicker to apprehend them and more likely they will be arrested and possibly charged (analysis and response). However, this is a reactive measure and may not do anything to reduce the crime issues in the interim and may simply result in displacement.

- Dedicated increased patrols throughout the night may be an effective visual deterrent but are unlikely to be feasible in terms of officer availability and resources. They are also unlikely to be the most effective use of police patrol time, as evidenced in the studies discussed above (Koper, 1995; Williams and Coupe, 2017).

- Officer patrols at the specific time where the problem is most experienced, in combination with the targeted intervention of drugs dogs, is likely to be the most effective policing response. It could serve as a visual deterrent, particularly if the patrols are limited to 10–15-minute periods; however, it may not be time effective for the officers to patrol for a short duration and then return to the area. It also depends upon the availability of drugs dogs at that time.

- Increased security personnel are not only likely to provide an additional deterrent for the club, but they will also be able to share information with the police, which will allow you to focus your resources on where would be most effective.

SAMPLE ANSWERS

REFLECTIVE PRACTICE 2.2

Skills you have gained which may be useful include: researching skills which can help you understand the evidence-base for different interventions, data analysis skills which can help evaluate the interventions; conducting primary research which can help you practice communicating with local citizens for the purpose of information gathering; as well as working as part of a team to problem-solve as you will have done during group work tasks.

REFLECTIVE PRACTICE 2.3

Answers may include communicating in advance with residents that they should expect an increased police presence as a result of the increased spate of burglaries, which may help assure citizens that the police are there to protect them. While conducting patrols, officers should engage with citizens and seek to understand their concerns and explain what the police are doing to assist. You could also engage with the local Pakistani community and faith leaders and seek their support in reassuring citizens. Engagement could also be coupled with advice as to preventative measures.

REFLECTIVE PRACTICE 2.4

- By providing a thorough explanation as to the grounds for suspicion and the basis for the stop. Actively listen to the citizens' comments and concerns and give them an opportunity to participate in the encounter by asking if they wish to provide their own version of events. You could display trustworthy motives by exhibiting care and concern for the safety of the local community and explain that searches are being conducted in response to the increased drug use and associated disorder. You should also treat the males with dignity and respect throughout the encounter, avoiding making any assumptions or being rude, impolite or sarcastic.

CHECK YOUR KNOWLEDGE

1. Hot spot policing entails the adoption of crime prevention strategies in micro-areas where reported crime and disorder is high.

2. Answers may include:

    - increased foot patrols;
    - the use of POP strategies;
    - increased reliance upon enforcement strategies such as stop and search and arrests;
    - the use of surveillance technologies such as CCTV and ANPR;
    - implementing situational crime prevention strategies.

3. The maximum time for foot patrols to be conducted is 10–14 minutes.

4. Focusing policing activity in hot spot locations risks moving crime to other locations. However there is limited evidence to suggest this occurs as a result of hot spot policing.

5. The procedural justice model suggests that if you treat citizens with dignity and respect, actively listen to them, explain the powers you are using and what you're doing in a manner which demonstrates neutrality, and you demonstrate trustworthy motives then citizens are more likely to be satisfied with a search encounter.

CHAPTER 3

REFLECTIVE PRACTICE 3.1

Scenario 1 – using the four-stage model, you may have considered practical solutions such as improved lighting (both fixed and motion sensors), increased fencing to restrict access to play equipment, warning signs to deter criminal behaviour and data-driven targeted approaches for police patrols and operations.

Scenario 2 – in this example, the data received will support the planning and operational aspects of the task. There is the need for the police to react quickly to the incident but they will need to liaise with other departments and third-party organisations such as Women's Aid or ManKind Initiative to ensure that support measures are in place both at the time of the incident and in the future. Extra consideration will be needed if there is the involvement of children or vulnerable people.

REFLECTIVE PRACTICE 3.3

- People at greater risk may include the homeless, young people, asylum seekers, the elderly and past victims of crime.

- Organisations and businesses at greater risk could include smaller independent shops, as well as high street chains. Shops with high-value items that are easy to move or sell, such as electronics, bicycles and motor vehicles, plus businesses in more remote locations may be subject to vandalism, break-ins and arson attempts.

- Locations that may be considered riskier could include parks, play areas, areas with reduced lighting and poor visibility, and areas with condensed numbers such as nightclubs, bars and pubs and car parks.

- Crime mapping serves a few key purposes:

    - it gives citizens an understanding of the types and locations of crimes in a particular area;

    - it provides the police and other law enforcement agencies with capacity to visualise and analyse crime patterns;

    - it supports resource deployment and future planning efforts for the police

CRITICAL THINKING ACTIVITY 3.2

The case of the Grindr Killer is an example of the most significant rape/murder investigations in recent history and explores how a new breed of killer can access victims via online dating applications. It showcases how the police can make mistakes when carrying out their work and how missed links, in this instance the locations of the four murder victims, allowed them to overlook information that would have supported their investigation. If geographic profiling methods (see below) had been applied to the investigation, it is *possible* that quicker conclusions may have been drawn and Stephen Port could have been apprehended earlier.

Geographic profiling is an investigative support technique that analyses data surrounding a connected series of crimes (often tied to serial killings) to try and determine the likely locations in which the offender lives/carries out their activities. Geographic profiling determines two key offender types: 1) *marauder* – operating in an area close to home and 2) *commuter* – travelling outside of their normal activity spaces to commit crime. Stephen Port would have been categorised as a marauder as the murders were all in close proximity to his home address.

REFLECTIVE PRACTICE 3.4

Predictive policing is a proactive policing model that utilises a range of gathered crime data and statistics, combined with algorithms and numerical techniques to predict where criminal activities may occur. It is usually linked to the short term and is used by the police as a tool to help them decide where to send resources. Other important aspects of predictive policing include the following.

- It supports the police with developing intervention and prevention strategies and tactics.

- It allows better planning and deployment of resources to locations where they are most needed.

- The four-phase cycle illustrates how organisations can utilise predictive policing in the support of the work they carry out – of particular note is the final phase, which focuses on the reflection and learning of the intervention.

- Predictive policing is concerned with location-based and person-based predictions and can determine both the potential location of a crime, as well as individuals or groups who are most at risk of becoming an offender *or* a victim.

- The model occasionally lacks the human element and therefore may not offer additional support to individuals involved in criminality when they most need it.

- Predictive policing has been criticised for stating the obvious – the same sort of crime often occurs in the same location – for example, train stations, football grounds or nightclubs.

CHECK YOUR KNOWLEDGE

1. Two core features of predictive policing are as follows.

   a) The use of a wide range and variety of data to support the police with the planning and deployment of resources. Data can be used from numerous policing databases, alongside other complementary organisations such as social services.

   b) A connection with pre-emptive policing that allows police services to act before criminal activities may take place. In this instance, predictive policing allows officers to be forward focused, rather than simply reacting to an event and having to deal with the consequences and repercussions.

2. The four phases of the predictive policing cycle are:

   a) **Data collection** – use of a wide range of data from relevant sources, ranging from basic data, such as the location of where a crime occurred, to more complex data, such as data linked to county lines offences.

   b) **Analysis and prediction** – in this phase you should be considering the types of crime that you want to target. These could be high-profile/risk crimes such as terrorism-related criminality to low-level but high-volume crimes such as drunk and disorderly incidents during the festive period.

c) **Police intervention** – who will you deploy to your incident? You should make your decision based upon the data and intelligence that has been gathered, alongside available resources and staff with necessary specialisms and skillsets.

d) **Target response** – this is your opportunity to reflect. Did your means of tackling the incident work or may there be a follow-up or knock-on impact from your deployment of resources? If there has been, how will you learn from this or mitigate the same things from happening in the future?

3. Benefits of predictive policing include: a greater ability to deploy resources to an area that is at risk from criminality, identification of individuals who may be involved in crime (both victims and offenders) and the ability to draw from a wide range of data (different crime types/offender information/gang affiliations/different welfare and supporting services) that can support the work of the police. Limitations of predictive policing include: lack of human interaction (not getting to the root cause of the issue), it is driven by data so there is the potential to have skewed (biased) information, plus it is said to predict the obvious in the sense that certain crimes will always happen in certain areas.

4. The three main ways of collecting data are routine collection, tasked information and volunteered information.

5. Your ideas may include ideas such as the ability to pinpoint locations that have a high degree of criminality (such as a shopping centre or outside of a nightclub) and how you may choose to task officers to those areas, especially on certain days/times when the level of crime may be higher. You could also use information such as this to inform local businesses and residents about simple crime prevention tips and safety advice, in order to better mitigate against the potential for crime to happen.

6. It is possible that predictive policing techniques may highlight an individual who could be classified as 'high risk', for example, a teenager who has been arrested on a number of occasions for petty crimes. Predictive policing will correctly flag the fact that the individual is at risk but may never address the underlying cause of their actions. In this scenario, the teenager may have been caught stealing to provide some form of financial aid for their family or they may have some form of gang involvement and need support to get out. Therefore, the role of the police isn't to simply arrest but to find additional ways to mitigate the impact to the individual and offer support and opportunity away from their current actions.

CHAPTER 4

REFLECTIVE PRACTICE 4.1

This may be deciding to lie when asked why you failed to do something, for example saying you were late to school owing to a traffic accident on your road instead of the truth that you overslept. It may be that you briefly considered what you wanted to convey (that you weren't responsible) and that you considered that you could have been in trouble with a teacher for telling the truth but escaped this by lying and choosing to lie. You may also feel like you didn't think this through but just acted under stress. You may recall that past experiences, fear of consequences or loss of the teacher's respect swayed your decision. You may then consider how you would respond as an officer if you had made a mistake (for example, failing to update notes) and consider what the implications of following a cost-benefit analysis as opposed to the Code of Ethics could be. You may decide that in your policing career when the stakes are higher, you'd be more likely to panic and respond with bounded rationality. Alternatively, you may think that you'd think things through more carefully as an officer, knowing that there could be serious implications for making the wrong decision.

CRITICAL THINKING ACTIVITY 4.1

- The law, social pressure from friends and family, rules at work and university, fear of family disapproval, social conditioning which stops us from disobeying cultural taboos (very few of us would board a busy train in pyjamas).

- The Code of Ethics, legislation, fear of public backlash, accountability measures such as scrutiny panels or fear of IOPC intervention, mechanisms for monitoring such as bodycam footage and CCTV.

- Police presence provides a deterrent, so during rational deliberation citizens may consider the likelihood of arrest or subsequent detection; this would dissuade them. Conversely, if the police are widely considered incompetent, a would-be offender may be more likely to risk committing crime.

CRITICAL THINKING ACTIVITY 4.2

Draw upon the bullet points on pages 74 and 75. An example answer may be:

There are lots of elements the police cannot control. However, they can change the environment, either by being more visible and acting as a deterrent or by using technology (such as CCTV) to achieve the same effect. They may also use communication via public information campaigns which either remind Nisha to be careful and thus render her less vulnerable or remind Mike of the possible consequences of mugging. Police could also inadvertently prevent this crime by arresting the loan shark and removing the motivation to offend.

CRITICAL THINKING ACTIVITY 4.3

- Young people pressured into criminality by peers, encountered in county lines operations.

- Those addicted to drugs: offenders who have committed burglaries to feed a habit.

- Victims of coercive control, who have been pressured to assist a partner's offending (such as handling stolen goods for them).

- People experiencing mental health problems, who may have intimidated members of the public, often unintentionally.

CRITICAL THINKING ACTIVITY 4.4

You may approach this question in any number of ways; below are three examples of possible answers you may give.

SUGGESTION 1

- I feel Sally committed murder. Yes, she was coercively controlled but she also monitored her husband's phone and tried to control him, so this seems to be a mutually abusive relationship. She chose to leave him and then begged to return; this means she was not trapped. She was logical enough to leave. She had a lot of time when travelling to kill him to consider her decision and was calm when talking to the police; this suggests she was able to rationally deliberate and the murder was out of jealousy, anger and revenge. People are victim-blaming when they say she isn't guilty: You can't say a man should die for being a bad husband! The only evidence that he raped or physically harmed her came from the woman who killed him.

- My values come from my parents; they taught me right from wrong and that two wrongs don't make a right. I was always punished for wrongdoing but rewarded if I admitted my faults and apologised before much harm was done. I think the media (social media, films, streaming services and TV) gives the same message as my parents.

SUGGESTION 2

- I don't think Sally can be at all legally responsible for what she did. She had been groomed by Richard – she was a child and he was a grown man when he began a relationship with her. She had never been an independent adult because she went from her parents making her decisions to her husband doing it. He made sure she didn't know how to cope on her own so when she left, she couldn't really survive. She only went back because he conditioned her into thinking she'd always be dependent, so he was all she had. When she knew he'd just betrayed her (again), she lost the ability to reason because it was so traumatic; he violated her emotionally, psychologically and sexually and he just got away with it. She just snapped; she couldn't take responsibility because she had never been allowed to so she couldn't control her emotions and she lost rationality. She can't be held criminally culpable.

- My morality comes mostly from my faith. In my religion we acknowledge that humans are flawed; we must all try our best, but people are weak, and we need God's power and guidance. It is also important to show forgiveness and compassion to those who have been unfortunate. The more we do that, the more we please God. My friends are also of the same faith as me and they agree with this; it is how we were all raised and when I see how we resolve any disagreements and compare it to how other people my age do (not to be judgemental), it is very different! I think focusing on the greater good and seeing everything through a lens of compassion is much more mentally and spiritually healthy.

SUGGESTION 3

- Sally is clearly guilty of manslaughter. She has been very honest about that; I admire her for it because a lot of people want to deny that she did anything wrong at all, but she admits that she did, which is very brave and makes me even more certain she is safe to be out of prison. She was put in a horrible situation; her husband sounds awful and everyone who knew them seems to corroborate her claims, at least in some way. However, she was not psychotic when she killed Richard; yes, she was coercively controlled and manipulated but she showed planning and consideration when carrying out the crime and in the aftermath. She had a lot of mitigation: after being groomed, abused, humiliated, mocked and then betrayed again, of course she wasn't thinking completely clearly but she did have bounded rationality. Her reasoning was impeded by her distress and the impacts of coercive control, but she retained the capacity to make decisions. She hadn't 'lost her mind' but she did have diminished responsibility so she's not fully culpable for murder, just manslaughter.

- My morals were formed at school. Not in a good way! We were treated very unfairly; my school was strict, and you were punished really severely for small things like talking in class! Then they tried to gaslight us by saying we had 'effectively signed a contract' by going to the school. It was the local school, we were children, we did not ask to be born there and we did not agree to their rules. One of my friends was bullied; the teachers just ignored it basically (except one or two nice ones but they always left) and the headteacher said that my friend was 'not helping himself' because he was openly gay. We all knew that basically they just didn't have the skills to tackle the problem, so they just let it carry on and because he was isolated and it wasn't an LGBT+ supportive community. I think my morals are also informed by growing up in such a narrow-minded area; I really do understand how big an impact feeling vulnerable can have on a person's mental health. The bullying and homophobia just continued because he was not going to get the support needed to fight back. So since then, I hate bullies, unfairness and people who take advantage of other people's vulnerability. But I also think it's wrong not to acknowledge your own responsibility for things; even if a situation is difficult, if you have a choice and you make the wrong one, you need to admit it.

REFLECTIVE PRACTICE 4.2

SCENARIO 1

- You could ask the university to improve lighting in the area.

- You could increase police presence and visibility.

- You could also hold a public meeting, providing security advice to students, and put up posters soliciting information to let everyone know that the police are actively investigating.

- You could provide students with stickers to put in their windows which suggest they are connected to a community home security group.

SCENARIO 2

- You could approach the man of Indian heritage and question him because you have intelligence from a witness that he may very loosely fit the description of the man you're looking for, but the description is vague and possibly inaccurate; you may worry about the dismissive way your white witness described other ethnic backgrounds, implying there is no real distinction to be made.

Not only does this question the credibility of the description (she also acknowledges she didn't see him closely) but may suggest she could be influenced by her own bias – her views on race may have made her expect this person not to be white; she is the only person to suggest he is not. The man at the club isn't exhibiting the behaviour of the suspect you're looking for. You could be accused of racial profiling.

- You could approach the white man who is alone and question him. The description is very vague, and he is possibly waiting for something; however, you may think it unethical to approach him when he doesn't fit the eyewitness description.

- You could quietly watch and wait: the suspect has never seriously assaulted anyone, and his behaviour reportedly escalates (from muttering, to ranting, to yelling, to shoving) so you should have time to prevent any physical violence. However, if you are wrong and today he is more aggressive than usual (perhaps if his delusions have changed), then someone could be hurt.

- You could make your presence very clear, walking up to and talking with people, allowing them to see an officer is present. This should hopefully deter any harassment. However, if the person is psychotic, it may not do this as he may not be able to make a rational deliberation but if he behaves aggressively, you can intervene. The main limitation with this strategy is that if your presence is all that deters him, he may go on to intimidate people again – you cannot be outside every club in the local area, all night, every night.

REFLECTIVE PRACTICE 4.3

- SAT would suggest changing the environment in Scenario 1: you could put in extra lighting; RAT would also approve this. For Scenario 2, you could ensure your presence is a deterrent to provide a suitable guardian for club-goers, as suggested by RAT.

- In both cases, you change the inputs and increase the deterrent element.

- In Scenario 1, burglaries decrease and confidence among students increases; however, this may only be temporary as offenders may learn to operate in locations where they are less likely to be observed (where people are asleep or are playing loud music meaning that offenders won't be disturbed, when people are in lectures etc) and thus simply adapt. In Scenario 2, either the suspect will not appear to behave in an intimidating way or if he does, you can arrest him and signpost him to whatever help he needs. However, if he isn't arrested that night, you won't know whether he will act again in the future or not.

- You may recall spates of burglaries or situations where mentally ill suspects have frightened the public.

- You could be accused of prejudice, inaction, causing panic, frustrating the public with inaction, you may not resolve the issue, you may make a member of the public feel targeted.

- In Scenario 1, students may become so worried that they move out or take the law into their own hands. In Scenario 2, you could be accused of harassment, racial profiling or neglecting public safety.

- See other answers to: What actions would the principles of RCT guide you towards? (Either RAT or SAT.)

- In all examples given thus far, the outcomes is a loss of public trust.

- Refer to one of the other examples, given above.

- You may choose to take any course of action discussed above, as long as you can explain why it is most likely to succeed.

- Least harm to the public and not causing panic; for Scenario 2 also not harming a vulnerable person.

- You are making use of the idea of deterrence with the aim of changing the environment to promote this.

CHECK YOUR KNOWLEDGE

1. To deter crime in order to decrease public pain and provide maximum pleasure for the population.

2. **Example:** You may not have secured the career you wanted if you had participated in low-level offending.

3. Utilitarianism aids deterrence and provides reassurance.

4. **Examples:** Stealing low-cost items; committing crime when you have a comfortable life, including a job you may lose if you gain a criminal record.

5. Learning disabilities kept his mental age at 11; he couldn't understand the significance of things he was told or understand long-term consequences as well as an adult would.

6. **Examples:** Mental health, age, cognitive differences (alter language, get an appropriate adult, seek expert advice). Substance abuse (provide food, rest and water, keep checking on the person and then reassess if they can be interviewed).

7. **Suggestions:** It is a necessary tool; it deters criminality and reassures the public. **Or:** It makes things worse; it cannot be used rationally as it is difficult to have criteria for success. It decreases public trust.

CHAPTER 5

CRITICAL THINKING ACTIVITY 5.1

Crime prevention is necessary as it reduces the risks of crimes occurring, and thus, the potential impact and effects on individuals, families, organisations and businesses. A sustained focus from the police on crime prevention helps to mitigate the emotional and physical damage to victims, alongside the financial impact of crime.

REFLECTIVE PRACTICE 5.1

Sample answers under each of the five main headings may include:

1. **Increase the effort**

    Security tags; facial recognition; biometric scanners.

2. **Increase the risk**

    Ring/smart doorbells; recommended services – those that have been officially vetted, for example Trustatrader; engage with friends and neighbours – make them aware if you are going to be away from your home.

3. **Reduce the rewards**

    Subtle branding of expensive products; disrupt the market for stolen goods; clearly identify property – this increases its ability to be spotted and makes the product less appealing to sell on.

4. **Reduce provocations**

    Improve services - better trained and more polite staff may limit the number of dissatisfied customers; respond to complaints – take complaints seriously and deal with them in a respectful manner; neutralise peer pressure – this is appliable to both young people and adults.

5. Remove excuses

Set rules and stick to them – an alcohol-free zone, should always be alcohol free; post clear instructions for people to follow, so they cannot state they didn't know what to do; add an extra layer of compliance – for example including a phone number and small deposit for restaurant bookings.

CRITICAL THINKING ACTIVITY 5.2

Level 5 answers may include:

- Other models you may have considered include problem-oriented policing, intelligence-led policing and zero-tolerance policing.

Level 6 answers may include:

- Hot spot policing focuses on concentrated areas of crime and is most effective when dealing with criminality linked to drug and disorder offences, as well as violent crime. It allows for the targeting of certain areas that are more prone to crime and is often driven via data and intelligence gathered through organisations. It allows decision makers to target resources at specific locations (those with the highest levels of crime), and if successful should lower the crime levels in a broader geographic location. Some studies suggest it does not tackle the underlying causes of crime and may simply displace crime to a new area. Hot spot policing is quite resource intensive and fewer numbers of deployable officers means that the operations may not have the hoped-for impact.

CRITICAL THINKING ACTIVITY 5.3

Suggestions may include:

- Where possible, keep items safely stored away and out of sight. For example, keep mobile phones in pockets/bags when not in use, particularly in communal areas/areas with high volumes of people.

- Consider if you need to take items with you everywhere, if not, leave them at home/work where they will likely be safer.

- Consider purchasing specific products that are designed to be more secure and safer to store items in them - for example rucksacks that zip from the back and not the front, reducing the opportunity for someone walking behind to unzip the bag and steal contents. Other items such as strong locks and high-decibel alarms are safer ways to protect items such as bikes and scooters.

- Cheaper alternatives should also be considered - for example cycling to school/college/work on a £100 bike rather than one that is worth thousands, may make it a less valuable target and therefore less likely to be stolen.

- Consider taking out insurance cover for items of high value - there is a cost associated with this decision but may be worth it in the long-term.

Challenges faced by the police may include:

- When a new hot product enters the market (for example escooters), quite soon after the item is replicated and copied in high numbers due to the popularity and scope for businesses to make money. It is at this point, where the police may face challenges, as it is likely that theft rates will climb rapidly as the opportunity to steal the item will significantly increase.

- An increase in the number of 'hot products' being stolen may drive the number of police calls and reports up, thus potentially challenging police resources.

- Theft of bags and rucksacks may contain a number of hot products, such as money, mobile phones, laptops and driving licences, which could be moved on to a range of different people, making it far harder to track down.

- Some hot products are consumable, for example vapes refills, so it is difficult for the police to determine if they have been stolen or not.

CRITICAL THINKING ACTIVITY 5.4

Practical crime reduction strategies could include:

- measures such as putting high-value items closer to CCTV cameras and security staff;

- additional alarms, security tags and locks to protect items from easy theft;

- higher-value products within locked cabinets;

- increased staffing during busy periods;

- increased warning signs;

- restricted entry/exit points;

- better barriers and fencing;

- greater number and deployment of security staff for larger areas;

- improved radio communication for staff.

REFLECTIVE PRACTICE 5.3

Sample solutions could include:

- addition of more lighting (both fixed and motion sensors);

- inclusion of CCTV cameras (though with significant cost attached);

- warning signs to potentially deter offenders;

- improved fencing and barriers;

- restricting access points;

- smoke alarms;

- additional office space such as a portacabin that can be staffed during busier periods.

It is worth considering that while there may be an additional cost of implementing some of your ideas such as adding CCTV cameras and strengthening barriers, the initial outlay may be significantly less than the continued cost of maintenance and repair. You should also consider that if there is no easy resolution to the problem, then the organisations may need to become more creative, be willing to invest, or take steps to manage their own spaces better.

CHECK YOUR KNOWLEDGE

1. Everyone – crime prevention is not simply down to the police to fix. Everyone has a chance to take steps and implement measures to reduce the chances of crime occurring. This can be from simple measures such as a bike owner storing a bike away from passers-by and utilising one or more locks to secure it to a fixed support, to the police and crime commissioner detailing the latest police and crime prevention plan.

2. Sample answers may include increased use of video doorbells, annual updates of ID cards and lanyards (each year the lanyards could be a different colour) and greater use of dashcams.

3. Concealable, removable, available, valuable, enjoyable, disposable.

4. Hot spots, hot victims, hot offenders and hot products – they are classified as 'hot' as they are either more desirable in the case of products, or at greater risk in the case of victims and spots.

5. Situational crime prevention is focused on the setting where crime occurs, such as a shopping centre, rather than on the people who look to commit crime. Situational crime prevention works by making it too difficult to commit crime, for example by adding more CCTV cameras, which makes an offender think again about trying to carry out their actions.

6. Sample answers could include better street lighting, barriers and bollards to direct footfall flow, addition of appealing features such as flowers and planting, better maintenance and upkeep of public areas – repairing damage and quickly removing graffiti.

7. Project Champion failed for several reasons, but its ultimate downfall was the lack of understanding of the impact at a local and community level and its ringfencing of a largely Muslim population. The initial proposal that had been put forward to local councillors was that its purpose was to reduce general crime and disorder and not that it was a surveillance operation linked to counterterrorism matters.

CHAPTER 6

REFLECTIVE PRACTICE 6.1

- Human trafficking: impacts a lot of people globally but probably not British nationals on the same scale as some other nations.

- Terrorism: impacts most people at least indirectly through fear and greater security measures.

- International fraud: very serious but doesn't directly impact most people but ramifications can cause international financial issues.

    - International co-operation is important to solve transnational crime, so this is positive. **Or:** It is concerning as different countries have different rules so another nation shouldn't interfere with how other people want to live, including how they enforce law and order.

SAMPLE ANSWERS

- I am pleased that criminals who have caused serious harm can't just move abroad and hurt someone else. **Or:** I worry that it involves the UK tracking down people who have disobeyed laws we wouldn't agree with or acting for corrupt or incompetent police forces who may have the wrong people. I also worry about UK citizens being found and detained by police who don't follow the same Code of Ethics as we do.

- The list seems to be reasonable; it is good that vulnerable people are a major concern and cybercrime can be very serious and bring down governments. Also it isn't interfering in other nation's politics; these are all issues all nations would want to resolve. **Or:** I don't think cybercrime should be as a high a priority as things like human trafficking: that seems out of place on the list. **Or:** With the rise of violent misogyny and far right movements, I think that violence against women and minority groups and the indoctrination which underpins it should be up there (even when it doesn't meet recognised criteria for terrorism).

- Charities; citizens; local authorities; the media.

- Some third sector organisations like the International Rescue Committee or Karma Nirvana have an international focus and may partner with other charities; others like Save the Children have branches across the world.

- Yes, they are an international law enforcement agency; they should comment on how member states' laws are enforced and if they think this is illegal by international law or even just immoral, they may be expected to help enforce such laws, so they have a right to an opinion. **Or:** No, the police shouldn't be politicised at all, and they have no right to try to influence the policies of a democratically elected government, especially as they are neither British nor elected.

- Yes, this is INTERPOL standing up for potentially vulnerable people so I agree they can comment but they shouldn't interfere on things like tax policy which won't directly impact them. **Or:** Yes, I'd have more sympathy with them interfering if it was something definitely outside international legal boundaries but not on this issue. **Or:** No, I would be happy for them to express views on anything, especially anything that impacts their work, for example Brexit. **Or:** No, I'd not ever be happy with them interfering.

- Yes, they have to be politically neutral or no one will work with them. **Or:** No, we shouldn't ever co-operate with dictators who oppress people. **Or:** They should look at the details and decide; if it's for what is internationally regarded as a genuine crime then, yes, but not if it seems political or to be religiously motivated oppression.

- **Pros:** Co-operation and information sharing; keeping people safe internationally; ensuring as many nations as possible co-operate with INTERPOL. **Cons:** Giving credibility to totalitarian governments; assisting political and religious oppression; giving information to dictators and corrupt law enforcement which could be used against innocent people.

- Loss of co-operation with those countries; loss of intelligence from them; dictators using it as an excuse for more oppressive criminal justice system policies; loss of intelligence on the oppression as the country becomes more isolated; loss of resources as that country withdraws (others may follow); this is also subjective as oppression means different things to different people and so it would be difficult to decide the criteria; inability to always determine if INTERPOL should act or not (just because it is a dictator accusing someone of a terrible crime doesn't mean it isn't true; conversely, oppressive governments may accuse opponents of serious offences and not admit that it is politically motivated).

- It means everyone will co-operate and they can effectively tackle crime in every country. Also, if they took a political stance, who would decide what this should be?

- No, those factors are always going to be important. **Or:** Yes, INTERPOL has been weaponised against political dissidents, and it can't allow that to continue.

- Countries may refuse to co-operate if governments won't assist them with their own concerns and they may stop letting INTERPOL have intelligence or let them into their nations to track down criminals.

CRITICAL THINKING ACTIVITY 6.1

- **Human trafficking:** exploitation, sexual violence, child abuse, physical and psychological harm; **Cybercrime:** financial harm for government and individuals, internet terrorism, non-contact sexual offending, organising serious offences; **Drugs:** exploitation, physical harm, crimes committed in connection with drug trafficking; **Illegal immigration:** possibility of criminals crossing state lines; **Counterfeiting of euros:** financial issues including inflation, money for organised crime gangs; **Money laundering:** money for organised crime, concealing offences which generated this money; **Gangs:** exploitation, violence, political corruption; **VAT fraud:** loss of tax revenue, money for organised crime; **Terrorism:** violence, intimidation of populations, radicalisation, exploitation; **Organised crime:** physical harms, political corruption, intimidation, exploitation; **Asset tracing:** losing track of fugitives, criminal groups and evidence; **Intellectual property offences:** loss of revenue for individuals and governments, exploitation, money for criminal activity; **Cigarette smuggling:** harm of smoking, loss of tax revenue, money for organised crime.

- **Terrorism:** For – it does a lot of harm. Against – countries have different types of threats and work with INTERPOL on this: is Europe-wide co-operation really necessary? **Smuggling of cigarettes:** For – this can fund organised crime. Against – these are legal substances and loss of tax revenue is not as severe an issue as terrorism or human trafficking.

- These work well with UK interests; Britain is concerned about terrorism etc too. **Or:** These are not consistent with UK interests; the euro is not British currency and VAT fraud is not as big an issue as violence against vulnerable people.

- Positive as the UK can organise relationships with countries as and when needed and can theoretically renegotiate the Working Arrangements with EUROPOL. **Or:** Negative as the UK has lost assurance of permanent frameworks for co-operation with the EU. There has been a decline in the relationship and the UK now has no ability to influence EUROPOL, which is answerable to the EU, meaning a key part of Britain's transnational crime strategy (the intelligence as well as some processes) will be influenced by other countries without any ability to mitigate this. The UK does not help set EUROPOL priorities, meaning they do not need to take British interests into account.

- See the examples above.

REFLECTIVE PRACTICE 6.1

- **Victim's right's campaigner:** By trying to ascertain if a conviction is likely or not, the CPS take away the ability for my client to ever get justice and leave them feeling disbelieved. The CPS cannot possibly know that the jury would not have believed them. The police believed my client and worked hard to get the evidence needed; we all feel it was enough.

- **Youth worker:** It is good that the CPS considers the public interest. My clients are very young, and it is not in anyone's interests to criminalise them just because the letter of the law says you can. Keeping young people out of young offenders' institutions and the criminal justice system in general benefits us all in the long run; they are more likely to lead productive lives and less likely to seriously offend in the future.

CRITICAL THINKING ACTIVITY 6.2

- The police do not necessarily understand how domestic violence and abuse impacts victims. They may need training so that they can empathise more and better deal with any barriers to co-operation and communication. Having this training also sends the right message and it is important to tackle a policing culture which was traditionally not sympathetic to victims of domestic violence and abuse.

- They do not have that negative history so people don't assume the worst of them; they aren't run by the state and don't have a uniform so may be less intimidating. Although officers can be victims of domestic violence and abuse, people often do not realise this and they are seen as symbols of resilience. Conversely, Women's Aid have survivors working for them, which may mean people expect to receive more empathy and understanding. Women's Aid also are focused on these issues and so service users will know that they see them as a priority unlike the police who have to balance competing concerns. Also, the police will be steering a victim towards a criminal justice system based solution, while Women's Aid can be more victim led.

REFLECTIVE PRACTICE 6.2

- Yes, these issues seep into children's behaviour in the community; also it is good for young people to see that there are consequences to actions but also view the police as approachable. **Or:** No, this could intimidate children and the school should be able to deal with such matters. Also, if we want the police to be a serious deterrent, they shouldn't be brought into trivial matters as this reduces the shock value.

- Given above.

- They get public money and have more powers to impact important factors; they have more resources and can be more easily regulated to ensure efficiency and ethical practice.

- Yes **or** No.

- I don't. **Or:** Schools and colleges because they deal with young people as well as anyone from the NHS and social services as they work with the most vulnerable and all these are well regulated and receive state funding.

- I don't. **Or:** Other organisations are only sometimes relevant, and you can't have too many organisations officially responsible or it makes it harder to determine who is truly in control and who is to blame for any mistakes.

CRITICAL THINKING ACTIVITY 6.3

- They tie in all relevant, responsible agencies and ensure a wide range of expertise is used.

- They are complex and it can be hard to determine where things went wrong as so many people are responsible; it is time-consuming and with staffing issues, stress and lack of resources, organisations may cut corners. The same organisations who make mistakes are the ones responsible for looking into how things went wrong and why.

- No, they should have more because they are elected. **Or:** No, they are not an expert and should just have a consultative role to help the police; decision making should be reserved for officers and government ministers. **Or:** Yes, it is the right balance of allowing the people a say and respecting democracy and acknowledging that expert opinion is sometimes the most important thing.

- **Examples:**

    - They are not legally binding and can just be dissolved. You don't need to be an expert and there is no official representation of civil rights groups etc to ensure the right questions are asked. The public don't pay them much attention.

    - They don't have legal powers but that is positive as it means non-experts who are directly impacted by policing policy can participate, similar to a jury. It means all officers know they could be subjected to scrutiny, helps the public understand policing policy, allows stakeholders (like youth workers) to participate and increases transparency.

- None. **Or:** It would send a message to the public that their input is not required or welcomed and would stop them from being able to feedback suggestions that would improve practice.

- Yes **or** No.

- Yes, there is no point in allowing scrutiny if it has no impact. If bad practice is shown to be systemic, then the panel should have the ability to legally demand change. **Or:** No, advice is great, but these are not experts. If you allowed this, you'd have to pour too much into training or change who could apply, which would decrease transparency; this would also get expensive.

CHECK YOUR KNOWLEDGE

1. To tackle international crime, apprehend dangerous fugitives, facilitate transnational information sharing and help tackle and gather data on threats to national and international security.

2. A Working Arrangement involving co-operation and sharing data but not helping EUROPOL set priorities.

3. The CPS considers the likelihood of successful conviction and the public interest.

4. Police, probation service, possibly prison service and domestic violence courts, safeguarding adults board, Children, School and Families, local authorities, fire and rescue services, social services and relevant NHS services.

5. Third sector organisations like Women's Aid, Victim Support, an IDVA and if there has been sexual violence possibly an ISVA. Depending on the victim's (or survivor's) identity, if relevant then community and/or faith-based support groups and specialist organisations such as those which focus on honour-based violence, LGBT+ victims or those with refugee status.

6. If there are children involved, school, social services and third sector specialists could support them.

7. Discussion at the domestic violence/abuse forum, a domestic homicide review and a Safeguarding Adult Review initiated by the safeguarding adults board.

REFERENCES

Alikhademi, K, Drobina, E, Prioleau, D, Richardson, B, Purves, D and Gilbert, J (2021) A Review of Predictive Policing from the Perspective of Fairness. *Artificial Intelligence and Law*, 30(1): 1–17.

Archer, B and Ellison, G (2023) *Police Procedure and Evidence in the Criminal Justice System*. St Albans: Critical Publishing.

Ariel, B (2022) Implementation Issues with Hot Spots Policing. Pre-print. [online] Available at: www.researchgate.net/publication/362593271 (accessed 10 March 2023).

Ariel, B, Weinborn, C and Sherman, L W (2016) 'Soft' Policing at Hot Spots: Do Police Community Support Officers Work? A Randomized Controlled Trial. *Journal of Experimental Criminology*, 12: 277–317.

Badiora, A and Adebara, O (2020) Residential Properties and Break-ins: Exploring Realtors and Residents' Perceptions of Crime Prevention through Environmental Design. *Property Management*, 38(3): 437–55.

Barlow, C and Walklate, S (2022) *Coercive Control*. London: Routledge.

Basford, L, Sims, C, Agar, I, Harinam, V and Strang, H (2021) Effects of One-a-day Foot Patrols on Hot Spots of Serious Violence and Crime Harm: A Randomised Crossover Trial. *Cambridge Journal of Evidence-based Policing*, 5: 119–33.

BBC News (2021) Households 'Buy 3.2 Million Pets in Lockdown'. *BBC News*, 12 March. [online] Available at: www.bbc.co.uk/news/business-56362987 (accessed 22 May 2023).

Beauregard, E and Martineau, M (2015) An Application of CRAVED to the Choice of Victim in Sexual Homicide: A Routine Activity Approach. *Crime Science*, 4(24): 1–11.

Beccaria, C (1995) *Beccaria: 'On Crimes and Punishments' and Other Writings*. Cambridge: Cambridge University Press.

Becker, G S (1968) Crime and Punishment: An Economic Analysis. *Journal of Political Economy*, 78: 169–217.

Beetham, D (1991) *The Legitimation of Power*. Basingstoke: Palgrave Macmillan.

Bentham, J (1983) *The Collected Works of Jeremy Bentham: Deontology. Together with a Table of the Springs of Action and the Article on Utilitarianism*. Oxford: Clarendon Press.

REFERENCES

Bettinson, V (2019) Aligning Partial Defences to Murder with the Offence of Coercive or Controlling Behaviour. *Journal of Criminal Law (Hertford)*, 83(1): 71–86.

Bottoms, A (2012) Developing Socio-Spatial Criminology. In Maguire, M, Morgan, R and Reiner, R (eds) *The Oxford Handbook of Criminology* (pp 450–89). Oxford: Oxford University Press.

Birmingham Police and Schools Panels (nd) About Police and Schools Panels. [online] Available at: https://policeandschools.org.uk/about.html (accessed 8 March 2023).

Bradford, B (2017) *Stop and Search and Police Legitimacy*. London: Routledge.

Bradford, B, Jackson, J and Stanko, A (2009) Contact and Confidence: Revisiting the Impact of Public Encounters with the Police. *Policing and Society*, 19(1): 20–46.

Braga, A and Weisburd, D (2010) *Policing Problem Places: Crime Hot Spots and Effective Prevention*. Oxford: Oxford University Press.

Braga, A, Papachristos, A and Hureau, D (2012) Hot Spots Policing Effects on Crime. *Campbell Systematic Reviews 2012*, 1: 1–96.

Braga, A A, Turchan, B S and Papachristos, A V (2019) Hot Spots Policing and Crime Reduction: An Update of an Ongoing Systematic Review and Meta-Analysis. *Journal of Experimental Criminology*, 15: 289–311.

Brayne, S, Rosenblat, A and Boyd, D (2015) Predictive Policing. In *Data and Civil Rights: A New Era of Policing and Justice*. [online] Available at: www.datacivilrights.org/pubs/2015-1027/Predictive_Policing.pdf (accessed 6 June 2023).

British Transport Police (2023) Together, We Can Stop Sexual Harassment. *Campaigns*. [online] Available at: www.btp.police.uk/police-forces/british-transport-police/areas/campaigns/Railway-Guardian (accessed 8 March 2023).

Bryant, R and Bryant, S (eds) (2019) *Blackstone's Handbook for Policing Students 2020*. 14th ed. Oxford: Oxford University Press.

Bullock, K and Leeney, D (2013) Participation, 'Responsivity' and Accountability in Neighbourhood Policing. *Criminology and Criminal Justice*, 13(2): 199–214.

Bullock, K and Tilley, N (2003) The Role of Research and Analysis: Lessons from the Crime Reduction Programme. *Crime Prevention Studies*, 15: 147–82.

Burke, R H (2019) Classical Criminology. In Hopkins, R (ed) *An Introduction to Criminological Theory* (pp 35–48). 5th ed. London: Routledge.

Care Act 2014 [online] Available at: www.legislation.gov.uk/ukpga/2014/23/contents/enacted (accessed 8 March 2023).

Chainey, S and Ratcliffe, J (2005) *GIS and Crime Mapping*. Chichester: John Wiley & Sons.

Chainey, S and Thompson, L (2012) Engagement, Empowerment and Transparency: Publishing Crime Statistics Using Online Crime Mapping. *Policing*, 6(3): 228–39.

Children Act 1989 [online] Available at: www.legislation.gov.uk/ukpga/1989/41/contents (accessed 8 March 2023).

Chiu, Y-N, Leclerc, B, Reynald, D and Wortley, R (2021) Situational Crime Prevention in Sexual Offenses Against Women: Offenders Tell Us What Works and What Doesn't. *International Journal of Offender Therapy and Comparative Criminology*, 65(9): 1055–76.

Chong, M D, Fellows, J and Kocsis, R (2018) Beyond Mere Deterrence: Rethinking Criminal Justice Policies for North Queensland. *James Cook University Law Review*, 24: 209–21.

Clarion Security Systems (2022) How Many CCTV Cameras Are in London? [online] Available at: https://clarionuk.com/resources/how-many-cctv-cameras-are-in-london (accessed 24 February 2023).

Clarke, R (1999) *Hot Products: Understanding, Anticipating and Reducing Demand for Stolen Goods*. Police Research Series Paper 112. London: Home Office.

Clarke, R V and Eck, J (2003) *Become a Problem-Solving Crime Analyst: In 55 Small Steps*. Jill Dando Institute of Crime Science. London: University College London.

Cohen, S (2011) *Folk Devils and Moral Panics: The Creation of the Mods and Rockers*. London: Routledge.

Cohen, L E and Felson, M (1979) Social Change and Crime Rate Trends: A Routine Activity Approach. *American Sociological Review*, 44: 588–605.

College of Policing (2018) *Neighbourhood Policing: Impact and Implementation: Summary Findings from a Rapid Evidence Assessment*. [online] Available at: https://assets.college.police.uk/s3fs-public/2021-02/np_rea_summary.pdf (accessed 8 March 2023).

College of Policing (2019) *Neighbourhood Policing Guidelines: Supporting Material for Frontline Officers, Staff and Volunteers*. [online] Available at: https://assets.college.police.uk/s3fs-public/2020-10/NPG_supporting_material_frontline%20(1).pdf (accessed 18 May 2023).

REFERENCES

College of Policing (2022) What Is Situational Crime Prevention? [online] Available at: www.college.police.uk/guidance/neighbourhood-crime/what-situational-crime-prevention (accessed 6 May 2023).

College of Policing (2023a) Neighbourhood Policing. [online] Available at: www.college.police.uk/guidance/neighbourhood-policing (accessed 9 March 2023).

College of Policing (2023b) Collection and Recording. [online] Available at: www.college.police.uk/app/information-management/management-police-information/collection-and-recording (accessed 23 February 2023).

College of Policing (2023c) Partnership Working and Multi-Agency Responses/Mechanisms. [online] Available at: www.college.police.uk/app/major-investigation-and-public-protection/domestic-abuse/partnership-working-and-multi-agency-responsesmechanisms (accessed 8 March 2023).

Cornish, D and Clarke, R (1987) Understanding Crime Displacement: An Application of Rational Choice Theory. *Criminology*, 25(4): 933–47.

Cornish, D and Clarke, R (2003) Opportunities, Precipitators and Criminal Decisions: A Reply to Wortley's Critique of Situational Crime Prevention. *Crime Prevention Studies*, 16: 41–96.

Cozens, P, Saville, G and Hillier, D (2005) Crime Prevention through Environmental Design (CPTED): A Review and Modern Bibliography. *Journal of Property Management*, 23(5): 328–56.

Crime and Disorder Act 1998 [online] Available at: www.legislation.gov.uk/ukpga/1998/37/section/6 (accessed 23 March 2023).

Crimestoppers (2023) Puppy Smuggling and Dog Theft. [online] Available at: https://crimestoppers-uk.org/news-campaigns/campaigns/puppy-smuggling-dog-theft (accessed 3 May 2023).

Criminal Justice Act 2003 [online] Available at: www.legislation.gov.uk/ukpga/2003/44/contents (accessed 8 March 2023).

Crown Prosecution Service (CPS) (2022a) Cautioning and Diversion. [online] Available at: www.cps.gov.uk/legal-guidance/cautioning-and-diversion (accessed 8 March 2023).

Crown Prosecution Service (CPS) (2022b) The Principles We Follow. [online] Available at: www.cps.gov.uk/principles-we-follow (accessed 8 March 2023).

Davenport, J (2010) Theresa May: Cut Crime as Well as Police Numbers. *London Evening Standard*, 15 September. [online] Available at: www.standard.co.uk/hp/front/theresa-may-cut-crime-as-well-as-police-numbers-6514039.html (accessed 3 July 2023).

Dearden, L (2018) Abuse victims describe the brutal reality of Thatcher's 'short, sharp shock' regime. *The Independent: Daily Edition*. [online] Available at: advance-lexis-com.bcu.idm.oclc.org/api/document?collection=news&id=urn:contentItem:5RG2-D3J1-F072-44YB-00000-00&context=1519360 [accessed 22 May 2023].

De Camargo, C (2020) 'They Wanna Be Us': PCSO Performances, Uniforms and Struggles for Acceptance. *Policing and Society*, 30(7): 854–69.

Domestic Violence, Crime and Victims Act 2004 [online] Available at: www.legislation.gov.uk/ukpga/2004/28/contents (accessed 8 March 2023).

Duggan, M (ed) (2018) *Revisiting the 'Ideal Victim'. Developments in Critical Victimology*. Bristol: Policy Press.

Eck, J E and Spelman, W (1987) Who Ya Gonna Call? The Police as Problem-busters. *Crime and Delinquency* 33(1): 31–52.

EUROPOL (2021) *Working and Administrative Arrangement Establishing Cooperative Relations between the Competent Authorities of the United Kingdom of Great Britain and Northern Ireland and the European Union Agency for Law Enforcement Cooperation*. [online] Available at: www.EUROPOL.europa.eu/cms/sites/default/files/documents/wa_with_united_kingdom_-_implementing_the_tca.pdf (accessed 8 March 2023).

EUROPOL (2022a) About EUROPOL. [online] Available at: www.EUROPOL.europa.eu/about-EUROPOL (accessed 8 March 2023).

EUROPOL (2022b) Agreements & Working Arrangements. [online] Available at: www.EUROPOL.europa.eu/partners-collaboration/agreements (accessed 8 March 2023).

Ewing, A C (1927) Punishment as a Moral Agency: An Attempt to Reconcile the Retributive and the Utilitarian View. *Mind*, 36(143): 292–305.

Ferguson, A (2017) Policing Predictive Policing. *Washington University Law Review*, 94(5): 1109–90.

Ferguson, L and Picknell, W (2022) Repeat or Chronic? Examining Police Data Accuracy across the 'History' Classifications of Missing Person Cases. *Policing and Society*, 32(5): 680–94.

REFERENCES

Fielding, M and Jones, V (2012) Disrupting the Optimal Forager: Predictive Risk Mapping and Domestic Burglary Reduction in Trafford, Greater Manchester. *International Journal of Police Science & Management*, 14(1): 30–41.

Fitz-Gibbon, K (2016) Minimum Sentencing for Murder in England and Wales: A Critical Examination 10 Years After the Criminal Justice Act 2003. *Punishment & Society*, 18(1): 47–67.

Gill, C, Weisburd, D, Telep, C W, Vitter, Z and Bennett, T (2014) Community-oriented Policing to Reduce Crime, Disorder and Fear of Increased Satisfaction and Legitimacy among Citizens: A Systematic Review. *Journal of Experimental Criminology*, 10(4): 399–428.

Goldstein, H (1979) Improving Policing: A Problem-oriented Approach. *Crime and Delinquency*, 25(2): 236–58.

Goold, B (2004) *CCTV and Policing: Public Area Surveillance and Police Practices in Britain*. Oxford Scholarship Online.

Gov.uk (2021) *Beating Crime Plan*. [online] Available at: https://assets.publishing.service.gov.uk/government/uploads/system/uploads/attachment_data/file/1015382/Crime-plan-v10.pdf (accessed 9 May 2023).

Gov.uk (2022) *Police Powers and Procedures: Stop and Search and Arrests, England and Wales, Year Ending 21 March 2022*. [online] Available at: www.gov.uk/government/statistics/police-powers-and-procedures-stop-and-search-and-arrests-england-and-wales-year-ending-31-march-2021 (accessed 28 February 2023).

Gul, S (2009) An Evaluation of Rational Choice Theory in Criminology. *Girne American University Journal of Sociology and Applied Science*, 4(8): 36–44.

Harris, J (2020) How Amazon Became a Pandemic Giant – and Why That Could Be a Threat to Us All. *The Guardian*, 18 November. [online] Available at: www.theguardian.com/technology/2020/nov/18/how-amazon-became-a-pandemic-giant-and-why-that-could-be-a-threat-to-us-all (accessed 9 May 2023).

Hayward, K (2007) Situational Crime Prevention and Its Discontents: Rational Choice Theory Versus the 'Culture of Now'. *Social Policy & Administration*, 41(3): 232–50.

Her Majesty's Inspectorate of Constabulary (HMIC) (2008) *Her Majesty's Inspectorate of Constabulary – Serving Neighbourhoods and Individuals*. London: HMIC. [online] Available at: www.justiceinspectorates.gov.uk/hmicfrs/media/serving-neighbourhoods-and-individuals-20081031.pdf (accessed 14 April 2023).

Her Majesty's Inspectorate of Constabulary and Fire & Rescue Services (HMICFRS) (2018) *Policing and Mental Health: Picking Up the Pieces*. [online] Available at: www.justiceinspectorates.gov.uk/hmicfrs/wp-content/uploads/policing-and-mental-health-picking-up-the-pieces.pdf (accessed 8 March 2023).

Higgins, A (2017) Core Functions: The Real Value of Neighbourhood Policing. The Police Foundation. [online] Available at: www.police-foundation.org.uk/2017/02/core-functions-the-real-value-of-neighbourhood-policing (accessed 12 March 2023).

Hinkle, J and Weisburd, D (2008) The Irony of Broken Windows Policing: A Micro-place Study of the Relationship between Disorder, Focused Police Crackdowns and Fear of Crime. *Journal of Criminal Justice*, 36(6): 503–12.

Home Office (2008) *From the Neighbourhood to the National: Policing Our Communities Together*. [online] Available at: https://assets.publishing.service.gov.uk/government/uploads/system/uploads/attachment_data/file/229019/7448.pdf (accessed 10 March 2023).

Hughes, G (1998) *Understanding Crime Prevention: Social Control, Risk and Late Modernity*. Buckingham: Open University Press.

Innes, M (2014) *Signal Crimes: Social Reactions to Crime, Disorder and Control*. Oxford: Oxford University Press.

Innes, M, Roberts, C, Lowe, T and Innes H (2020) *Neighbourhood Policing: The Rise and Fall of a Policing Model*. Oxford: Oxford University Press.

INTERPOL (2023a) About Red Notices. [online] Available at: www.INTERPOL.int/en/How-we-work/Notices/About-Red-Notices (accessed 8 March 2023).

INTERPOL (2023b) What Is INTERPOL? [online] Available at: www.INTERPOL.int/en/Who-we-are/What-is-INTERPOL (accessed 8 March 2023).

INTERPOL (2023c) United Kingdom. [online] Available at: www.INTERPOL.int/en/Who-we-are/Member-countries/Europe/UNITED-KINGDOM (accessed 8 March 2023).

Jacobs, J (2021) Has INTERPOL Become the Long Arm of Oppressive Regimes? *The Guardian*, 17 October. [online] Available at: www.theguardian.com/global-development/2021/oct/17/has-INTERPOL-become-the-long-arm-of-oppressive-regimes (accessed 8 March 2023).

Jansen, F (2018) *Data Driven Policing in the Context of Europe*. Cardiff University Working Paper. [online] Available at: https://datajusticeproject.net/wp-content/uploads/sites/30/2019/05/Report-Data-Driven-Policing-EU.pdf (accessed 28 February 2023).

REFERENCES

Joyce, P (2011) *Policing: Development & Contemporary Practice*. London: Sage Publications.

Kirby, S and Keay, S (2021) *Improving Intelligence Analysis in Policing*. Abingdon: Routledge.

Koper, C S (1995) Just Enough Police Presence: Reducing Crime and Disorderly Behavior by Optimizing Patrol Time in Crime Hot Spots. *Justice Quarterly*, 12(4): 649–72.

Lazzati, N and Menichini, A (2016) Hot Spot Policing: A Study of Place-Based Strategies for Crime Prevention. *Southern Economic Journal*, 82(3): 893–913.

Leese, M (2021) Security as Socio-Technical Practice: Predictive Policing and (Non-)Automation, *Swiss Political Science Association*, 27(1): 150–7.

Lister, S, Adams, B and Phillips, S (2015) *Evaluation of Police–Community Engagement Practices*. Swindon: Economic and Social Research Council.

Macbeth, E and Ariel, B (2019) Place-Based Statistical versus Clinical Predictions of Crime Hot Spots and Harm Locations in Northern Ireland. *Justice Quarterly*, 36(1): 93–126.

Mangan, L (2019) The Case of Sally Challen Review: Inside the Trial That Changed Everything for Women. *The Guardian*, 9 December. [online] Available at: www.theguardian.com/tv-and-radio/2019/dec/09/the-case-of-sally-challen-review-inside-the-trial-that-changed-everything-for-women (accessed 13 March 2023).

Mapping London (2013) Violent Crime Hotspots in London. [online] Available at: https://mappinglondon.co.uk/2013/violent-crime-hotspots-in-london (accessed 31 March 2023).

Mastrofski, S (1999) *Policing for People – Ideas in American Policing*. Washington, DC: Police Foundation.

McCahill, M (2002) *The Surveillance Web: The Rise of Visual Surveillance in an English City*. Abingdon: Willan Publishing.

McLaughlin, E and Muncie, J (eds) (2013) *Controlling Crime*. 2nd ed. London: Sage Publications.

McLaughlin, E and Muncie, J (eds) (2019) *The SAGE Dictionary of Criminology*. 2nd ed. London: Sage Publications.

Meijer, A and Wessels, M (2019) Predictive Policing: Review of Benefits and Drawbacks. *International Journal of Public Administration*, 42(12): 1031–9.

Mendelsohn, B (1976) Victimology and Contemporary Society's Trends. *Victimology*, 1(1): 8–28.

Merritt, J (2010) W(h)ither the PCSO? Police Perceptions of the Police Community Support Officer's Role, Powers and Future Directions. *Policing: An International Journal of Police Strategies and Management*, 33(4): 731–49.

Metropolitan Police (2022) Community-based Volunteers. [online] Available at: www.met.police.uk/car/careers/met/police-volunteer-roles/community-based-volunteers/overview (accessed 9 May 2023).

Meynen, G (2010) Free Will and Mental Disorder: Exploring the Relationship. *Theoretical Medicine and Bioethics*, 31(6): 429–43.

Moffat, R (1983) Crime Prevention through Environmental Design: A Management Perspective. *Canadian Journal of Criminology*, 25(4): 19–31.

Morash, M and Ford, J K (2002) *The Move to Community Policing: Making Changes Happen*. Thousand Oaks, CA: Sage Publications.

Moses, L and Chan, J (2018) Algorithmic Prediction in Policing: Assumptions, Evaluation, and Accountability. *Policing and Society*, 28(7): 806–22.

Myhill, A (2012) *Community Engagement in Policing: Lessons from the Literature*. London: Home Office.

Nagin, D S (1998) Criminal Deterrence Research at the Outset of the Twenty-first Century. *Crime and Justice*, 23: 1–42.

National Crime Agency (NCA) (2021) NCA and EUROPOL Sign Up to a New Working Arrangement. [online] Available at: https://nationalcrimeagency.gov.uk/news/nca-and-europol-sign-up-to-a-new-working-arrangement (accessed 8 March 2023).

National Institute of Justice (2014) Overview of Predictive Policing. [online] Available at: https://nij.ojp.gov/topics/articles/overview-predictive-policing (accessed 8 March 2023).

Neighbourhood Watch (2020) Crime Prevention. [online] Available at: www.ourwatch.org.uk/crime-prevention (accessed 14 May 2023).

O'Malley, P and Smith, G J (2022) 'Smart' Crime Prevention? Digitization and Racialized Crime Control in a Smart City. *Theoretical Criminology*, 26(1): 40–56.

O'Neill, M (2011) Policing Myths: Megan O'Neill Explores the Myth That Bobbies on the Beat Cut Crime. *Criminal Justice Matters*, 83(1): 32–3.

O'Neill, M (2014) Ripe for the Chop or the Face of Public Policing? *Policing: A Journal of Policy and Practice*, 8(3): 265–73.

Oliver, M and Agencies (2007) Home Office Denies INTERPOL Criticisms. *The Guardian*, 9 July. [online] Available at: www.theguardian.com/uk/2007/jul/09/terrorism.immigration policy (accessed 8 March 2023).

Olson, J, Martin, R L and Connell, N M (2021) Satisfaction with Life and Crime: Testing the Link. *Psychology, Crime & Law*, 27(7): 631–55.

Parris, J (1991) *Scapegoat: The Inside Story of the Trial of Derek Bentley*. London: Duckworth.

Paternoster, R (2010) How Much Do We Really Know about Criminal Deterrence? *Journal of Criminal Law and Criminology*, 100(3): 765–824.

Perry, W (2013) *Predictive Policing: The Role of Crime Forecasting in Law Enforcement Operations*. Santa Monica, CA: Rand Corporation.

Pierce, G, Spaar, S and Briggs, L (1988) *The Character of Police Work: Strategic and Tactical Implications*. Boston, MA: Centre for Applied Social Research, Northeastern University.

Police Foundation (2006) *Users' Guide to Mapping Software for Police Agencies*. 8th ed. Washington, DC: Crime Mapping and Problem Analysis Laboratory.

Police Foundation (2014) *The Briefing: Police Use of Social Media*. [online] Available at: www.police-foundation.org.uk/2017/wp-content/uploads/2017/08/Social_media_briefing_FINAL.pdf (accessed 28 February 2023).

Police Foundation (2015) *Neighbourhood Policing: Past, Present and Future*. [online] Available at: www.police-foundation.org.uk/2017/wp-content/uploads/2017/06/neighbourhood_policing_past_present_future.pdf (accessed 9 March 2023).

Police Reform Act 2002 [online] Available at: www.legislation.gov.uk/ukpga/2002/30/section/12 (accessed 8 March 2023).

Police Reform and Social Responsibility Act 2011 [online] Available at: www.legislation.gov.uk/ukpga/2011/13/section/3/enacted (accessed 8 March 2023).

Police.uk (2023) Automatic Number Plate Recognition (ANPR). [online] Available at: www.police.uk/advice/advice-and-information/rs/road-safety/automatic-number-plate-recognition-anpr (accessed 24 February 2023).

Quinton, P (2011) The *Impact of Information about Crime and Policing on Public Perceptions: The Results of a Randomised Controlled Trial*. London: National Policing Improvement Agency.

Quinton, P and Morris, J (2008) *Neighbourhood Policing: The Impact of Piloting and Early National Implementation*. London: Home Office.

Ratcliffe, J (2018) *Intelligence-led Policing*. 2nd ed. London: Routledge.

Regalado, J, Timmer, A and Jawaid, A (2022) Crime and Deviance During the COVID-19 Pandemic. *Sociology Compass*, 16(4): 1–17.

Rosenbaum, D P (2006) The Limits of Hot Spot Policing. In Weisburd, D and Braga, A A (eds) *Police Innovation: Contrasting Perspectives* (pp 314–46). Cambridge: Cambridge University Press.

Rowe, M (2018) *Introduction to Policing*. 3rd ed. London: Sage Publications.

Russell, P (2021) The Limits of Free Will: Replies to Bennett, Smith and Wallace. *Ethical Theory and Moral Practice*, 24(1): 357–73.

Sandhu, A and Fussey, P (2021) The 'Uberization of Policing'? How Police Negotiate and Operationalize Predictive Policing Technology. *Policing and Society*, 31(1): 66–81.

Sevigny, E and Zhang, G (2018) Do Barriers to Crime Prevention Moderate the Effects of Situational Crime Prevention Policies on Violent Crime in High Schools? *Journal of School Violence*, 17(2): 164–79.

Sherman, L, Gartin, P and Buerger, M (1989a) *Repeat Call Address Policing: The Minneapolis RECAP Experiment. Final Report to the National Institute of Justice*. Washington, DC: Crime Control Institute.

Sherman, L, Gartin, P and Buerger, M (1989b) Hot Spots of Predatory Crime: Routine Activities and the Criminology of Place. *Criminology*, 27: 27–56.

Simmonds, D (2015) *Why is the Clutch Slipping? Developing Clarity, Capacity and Culture for Citizen and Community Engagement*. National College of Policing.

Skogan, W G and Steiner, L (2004) *Community Policing in Chicago, Year Ten*. Chicago, IL: Illinois Criminal Justice Authority.

Smith, M J (2017) Rational Choice. In Brisman, A, Carrabine, E and South, N (eds) *The Routledge Companion to Criminological Theory and Concepts* (pp 87–91). 1st ed. London: Routledge.

South Yorkshire Police (SYP) (2022) Scrutiny Panel. [online] Available at: www.southyorks.police.uk/find-out/stop-and-search/scrutiny-panel (accessed 8 March 2023).

Spelman, W and Eck, J E (1989) Sitting Ducks, Ravenous Wolves, and Helping Hands: New Approaches to Urban Policing. *Public Affairs Comment*, 35: 1–9.

REFERENCES

Squires, P (ed) (2008) *ASBO Nation: The Criminalisation of Nuisance*. Bristol. Policy Press.

Statista (2022a) Number of Police Officers in England and Wales from 1979 to 2022. [online] Available at: www.statista.com/statistics/303973/police-officer-figures-england-and-wales (accessed 23 February 2023).

Statista (2022b) Number of Pet Dogs in the United Kingdom (UK) from 2010/11 to 2021/22 (in Millions). [online] Available at: www.statista.com/statistics/515379/dogs-population-in-the-united-kingdom-uk/ (accessed 9 May 2023).

Statista (2023) Number of Social Media Users Worldwide from 2017 to 2027. [online] Available at: www.statista.com/statistics/278414/number-of-worldwide-social-network-users (accessed 28 February 2023).

Steele, R (2015) How Offenders Make Decisions: Evidence of Rationality. *British Journal of Community Justice*, 13(3): 7–20.

Taylor, B, Koper, C and Woods, D (2011) A Randomised Controlled Trial of Different Policing Strategies at Hot Spots of Violent Crime. *Journal of Experimental Criminology*, 7: 149–81.

Thales (2022) A New Era Dawns for the British Passport. [online] Available at: www.thalesgroup.com/en/markets/digital-identity-and-security/government/customer-cases/uk-passport (accessed 9 May 2023).

The Conversation (2022) Artificial Intelligence Is Used for Predictive Policing in the US and UK: South Africa Should Embrace It, Too. [online] Available at: https://theconversation.com/artificial-intelligence-is-used-for-predictive-policing-in-the-us-and-uk-south-africa-should-embrace-it-too-191266 (accessed 9 May 2023).

Thomas, K J, Loughran, T A and Hamilton, B C (2020) Perceived Arrest Risk, Psychic Rewards, and Offense Specialization: A Partial Check of Rational Choice Theory. *Criminology*, 58(3): 485–509.

Tilley, N (2009) *Crime Prevention*. Cullompton: Willan Publishing.

Tuffin, R, Morris, J and Poole, A (2006) *An Evaluation of the Impact of the National Reassurance Policing Programme*. London: Home Office.

Turley, C, Raans, H M, Callanan, M, Blackwell, A and Newburn, T (2012) *Delivering Neighbourhood Policing in Partnership,* Research Report 61. [online] Available at: https://assets.publishing.service.gov.uk/government/uploads/system/uploads/attachment_data/file/116524/horr61.pdf (accessed 18 May 2023).

Tyler, T (2004) Enhancing Police Legitimacy. *The Annals of the American Academy of Political and Social Science*, 593(1): 84–99.

Von Hentig, H (1948) *The Criminal and His Victim: Studies in the Sociobiology of Crime*. New Haven, CT: Yale University Press.

von Lampe, K (2011) The Application of the Framework of Situational Crime Prevention to 'Organized Crime'. *Criminology & Criminal Justice*, 11(2): 145–63.

Wain, N, and Ariel, B (2014) Tracking of Police Patrol. *Policing: A Journal of Policy and Practice*, 8(3): 274–83.

Weisburd, D (2008) *Place-Based Policing*. Ideas in American Policing. Washington, DC: Police Foundation.

Weisburd, D and Majmundar, M (2018) *Proactive Policing: Effects on Crimes and Communities*. Washington, DC: The National Academies Press.

Weisburd, D, Wyckoff, L A, Ready, J, Eck, J E, Hinkle, J C and Gajewski, F (2006) Does Crime Just Move Around the Corner? A Controlled Study of Spatial Displacement and Diffusion of Crime Control Benefits. *Criminology*, 44: 549–92.

Weisburd, D, Telep, C W, Hinkle, J C and Eck, J E (2010) Is Problem-oriented Policing Effective in Reducing Crime and Disorder? *Criminology & Public Policy*, 9(1): 139–72.

Weisburd, D, Telep, C, Vovak, H, Zastrowa, T, Braga, A and Turchan, B (2021) Reforming the Police through Procedural Justice Training: A Multicity Randomized Trial at Crime Hot Spots. *Proceedings of the National Academy of Sciences of the United States of America*, 119(14): e2118780119.

Welch, B, Braga, A and Bruinsma, G (2015) Reimagining Broken Windows: From Theory to Policy. *Journal of Research in Crime and Delinquency*, 52(4): 447–63.

West Midlands Police (WMP) (nd) Support Agencies: Birmingham. [online] Available at: www.west-midlands.police.uk/domestic-abuse/supporting-agencies/birmingham (accessed 8 March 2023).

West Midlands Police (WMP) (2022) Police Drones. [online] Available at: www.west-midlands.police.uk/frequently-asked-questions/police-drones (accessed 28 February 2023).

West Midlands Police (WMP) (2023a) Stop and Search Scrutiny Panels. [online] Available at: www.westmidlands-pcc.gov.uk/tackling-violence/stop-search/stop-and-search-scrutiny-panels (accessed 8 March 2023).

West Midlands Police (WMP) (2023b) What Is a PCC? [online] Available at: www.westmidlands-pcc.gov.uk/your-commissioner/what-is-a-pcc (accessed 8 March 2023).

Wheeler, A P and Reuter, S (2021) Redrawing Hot Spots of Crime in Dallas, Texas. *Police Quarterly*, 24(2): 159–84.

Wikström P-O (2017) Character, Circumstances, and the Causes of Crime. In Liebling, A, Maruna, S and McAra, L (eds) *The Oxford Handbook of Criminology* (pp 501–21). Oxford: Oxford University Press.

Wikström, P-O (2018) Situational Action Theory. In Cullen, F T and Wilcox, P (eds) *Oxford Research Encyclopedia (ORE) of Criminology and Criminal Justice* (pp 1000–8). Oxford: Oxford University Press.

Wikström, P-O and Treiber, K (2018) The Dynamics of Change: Criminogenic Interactions and Life-course Patterns of Crime. In Farrington, D P, Kazemian, L and Piquero, A (eds) *The Oxford Handbook of Developmental and Life-course Criminology* (pp 272–94). Oxford: Oxford University Press.

Williams, B (2023) *Policing Mental Health, Vulnerability and Risk*. St Albans: Critical Publishing.

Williams, S A (2015) *Do Visits Spent in Hot Spots Patrol Matter Most? A Randomised Control Trial in the West Midlands Police*. Master's thesis. Cambridge: University of Cambridge.

Williams, S and Coupe, T (2017) Frequency vs Length of Hot Spot Patrols: A Randomised Controlled Trial. *Cambridge Journal of Evidence-based Policing*, 1: 5–21.

Wilson, J Q and Herrnstein, R (1985) *Crime and Human Nature*. New York: Simon & Schuster.

Wilson, J Q and Kelling, G L (1982) Broken Windows. In Bean, P (ed) *Crime: Critical Concepts in Sociology Vol 2* (pp 277–95). London: Routledge.

Women's Aid (2022) Police Training: Domestic Abuse Matters. [online] Available at: www.womensaid.org.uk/what-we-do/training/police-training (accessed 8 March 2023).

Wood, D (2020) *Towards Ethical Policing*. Bristol: Policy Press.

Zahm, D (2007) *Using Crime Prevention through Environmental Design in Problem-Solving*. [online] Available at: https://popcenter.asu.edu/sites/default/files/using_cpted_in_problem_solving.pdf (accessed 9 May 2023).

INDEX

Note: Page numbers in *italics* and **bold** denote figures and tables, respectively.

access control points, 103
activity support, 104
ANPR cameras, 54
antisocial behaviours, 34, 75–6
ASBOs, 75–6
asset tracing, 156

beat meetings, 14
Beating Crime Plan 2021, 28
bounded rationality, 67, 144
Broken Windows Theory, 7, 38, 104–6

Care Act 2014, 127
CCTV surveillance, 31, 54, 103, 108, 138
CHEERS, 39–40
Children Act 2004, 127
cigarette smuggling, 156, 157
collective efficacy, 8, 14–15, 134
Community Based Volunteers (CBV), 99
community engagement, 11–14, 99
  barriers of, 13
  social media in, 24
  stage of, *16*
community mapping, **14**
community partnership, 123–4
community policing, 2–3, 14–15
Community Safety Partnerships, 121
community tensions, 40–2
community-led approach, 18–19
co-production, 14–15

Cornish and Clarke's 25 techniques of crime prevention, 90–3
CRAVED model, 97–9
Crime and Disorder Act 1998, 124
crime mapping, 57–60, 141
crime mapping software, 32
crime prevention, 88–9, 150
  partnership, evaluation of, 124–7
  partnerships in, 114
  25 techniques of, 90–3
Crime Prevention Through Environmental Design (CPTED)
  application of, 102–3
  approach of, 102
  categories of, 103–4
crime reduction, practical strategies, 152–3
Criminal Justice Act 2003, 124
criminal justice system (CJS), 75
Crown Prosecution Service (CPS), 120–1, 157
cybercrime, 156

data acquisition/data management software, 60
data collection, 53–5, 143
Deterrence Theory, 31, 66
distraction burglary, 95
Domestic Homicide Reviews (DHRs), 125
Domestic Violence and Abuse (DVA), 125

domestic violence and abuse forums, 126–7
Domestic Violence, Crime and Victims Act 2004, 125
drones, use in policing, 55
drugs use, 156

emergency management software, 61
EUROPOL, *118*, 157
  and crime in UK, 120
  impact of Brexit on, 119
euros, counterfeiting of, 156

foot patrols, 7, 9, 10, 31, 34, 40

gangs, 156
geocoding, 60
geographic information system (GIS), 32, 56–7, 60–1
geographic profiling methods, 141

'high-visibility' policing, 34–5
hot offender, 96
hot products, 96–7
hot spot locations, 23, 29, 93–5, 136
  identification of, 32–3
  policing activities in, 30
hot spot policing, 7, 138, 151
  activities in, 33–4
  barriers in, 36
  definition of, 28
  strategies of, 28–31

INDEX

hot victims, 95
human trafficking, 154, 156

illegal immigration, 156
image/maintenance, of space, 103
information collection, 52-3
intellectual property offences, 156
intelligence-led policing (ILP), 56, 151
intensive enforcement, 7
international fraud, 154-6
internet mapping, 61
INTERPOL, 114-15
  and NCB of United Kingdom (UK), 115-16
  composition of, policy of neutrality in, 116-17

Koper Curve, 23-4

Local Crime and Justice Partnerships, 121
Local Safeguarding Children Boards (LSCB), 127

money laundering, 156
moral panics, 75, 76
Multi Agency Public Protection Arrangements (MAPPA), 121
Multi Agency Risk Assessment Conference (MARAC), 121

National Central Bureau (NCB), 114
National Reassurance Policing Programme (NRPP), 3-4

neighbourhood policing, 2, 136
  basic standards of, 5
  community priorities in, 15-17
  criteria, 5
  critical success factors of, 5
  evolution of, 4-5
  future of, 24
  impact of austerity on, 8-9
  models of, 6-8
  PCOs related issues in, 10-11
  principles of, 5-6
  vital aspects of, 11-23
Neighbourhood Watch, 15, 99

organised crime, 156

partner-led approach, 18
PEA hypothesis, 69, 71-2, 73-4
Police and Crime Commissioners (PCCs), 128
Police Community Support Officers (PCSOs), 9-11, 136
police legitimacy, lower perceptions of, 133
Police Reform Act 2002, 9
Police Reform and Social Responsibility Act 2011, 14, 128
predictive policing, 7-8, 46, 141-2, 143
  applications of, 49
  assessment of, 61-2
  benefits of, 50-1, 143
  controversies in, 50
  core features of, 47
  and databases, 46-7
  defining, 46
  ethical policing in, 61
  features of, 142
  limitations of, 51-2

phases of, 142-3
stages of, *48*
preventative patrols, 34-5
proactive policing, 55, 141-2
problem analysis triangle, *20*
problem-oriented policing (POP), 8, 36-40, 56, 151
  and SARA model, 37-8
  and zero-tolerance policing, 38
problem-solving strategy, 17
procedural justice model
  and neighbourhood policing, *17*
  and police-citizen encounters, 41-2
Project Champion, 109, 110, 154

randomised control trials (RCT), 21
Rational Choice Theory (RCT), 66
  and coercive control, 77-8, 79-80
  and community-based policing, 81-4
  critiques of, 77
  and individuality ignorance, 77-80
  influence on legislation, 76
  influence on policing practice, 76
  and mental disorders management, 77, 78-9
  origin of, 66-7
  and police legitimacy, 81
  and Routine Activity Theory, 67-9
  and Situational Action Theory, 69-70

red notices, 115
risk assessment, 140
Routine Activity Theory (RAT), 31, 67–9
routine collection, 52
routing software, 61

Safeguarding Adult and Children's Boards, 121–2
Safeguarding Adult Review (SAR), 127
Safeguarding Adults Boards (SABs), 127–8
Scanning, Analysis, Response, Assessment (SARA) model, 17–22
Scrutiny Panels, community-based, 128–9
'short, sharp shock' policy, 75
Situational Action Theory (SAT), 67, 69–70
activity field changes and, 73
activity for changes in, 74–5
changes in crime propensities, 72
personal changes and, 72
situational crime prevention (SCP), 154
and criminological theories, 100
definition of, 100
goals of, 100
measures, 100–2
products of, 106–8
surveillance technology used in, 108–10
social media platforms, 54
spatial crime displacement, 35
Specialist Domestic Violence Courts, 122
stop and search records, 54
street watch, 99
surveillance (formal and informal), 103

target hardening, 104
targeting activity, 23–4
tasked information, 53
territoriality, 103
terrorism, 154, 156, 157

utilitarian principles, 66

VAT fraud, 156
volunteered information, 53

Women's Aid, 122–3, 157–8

zero-tolerance policing, 7, 23, 38, 151